이디엄 속 세상 이야기
World History Inside Idioms

이디엄 속 세상 이야기
World History Inside Idioms

초판 1쇄 발행 2023년 5월 22일

지은이 서수진
펴낸이 장현수
펴낸곳 메이킹북스
출판등록 제 2019-000010호

디자인 박단비
편집 박단비
교정 강인영
마케팅 장윤정

주소 서울특별시 구로구 경인로 661, 핀포인트타워 912-914호
전화 02-2135-5086
팩스 02-2135-5087
이메일 making_books@naver.com
홈페이지 www.makingbooks.co.kr

ISBN 979-11-6791-358-6(13740)
값 23,000원

ⓒ 서수진 2023 Printed in Korea

잘못된 책은 구입하신 곳에서 바꾸어 드립니다.
이 책의 전부 또는 일부 내용을 재사용하려면 사전에 저작권자와 펴낸곳의 동의를 받아야 합니다.

홈페이지 바로가기

메이킹북스는 저자님의 소중한 투고 원고를 기다립니다.
출간에 대한 관심이 있으신 분은 making_books@naver.com으로 보내 주세요.

이디엄 속 세상 이야기
World History Inside Idioms

글&그림 **서수진 (Suzie Suh)**

메이킹북스

Contents

책머리에	6
Idioms from A to Z: A	11
Idioms from A to Z: B	21
Idioms from A to Z: C	35
Idioms from A to Z: D	51
Idioms from A to Z: E	64
Idioms from A to Z: F	80
Idioms from A to Z: G	102
Idioms from A to Z: H	120
Idioms from A to Z: I	140
Idioms from A to Z: J	154
Idioms from A to Z: K	170

Idioms from A to Z: L   183

Idioms from A to Z: M   198

Idioms from A to Z: N   216

Idioms from A to Z: O   229

Idioms from A to Z: P   236

Idioms from A to Z: Q   265

Idioms from A to Z: R   274

Idioms from A to Z: S   302

Idioms from A to Z: T   364

Idioms from A to Z: U, V   390

Idioms from A to Z: W   400

Idioms from A to Z: X, Y, Z   424

◎ 책머리에 ◎

이 책은 대부분의 영어 교수와 학습이 시험 대비를 위한 학문적(academic) 영어에 치우친 한국의 특수한 영어 교육 환경 속에서, 영어를 배우는 분들이 한국에서도 좀 더 진정성(authentic) 있게 영어 활용 능력을 향상시키는 데에 도움을 주고자 만들게 되었다.

실제 글쓴이가 미국에 있는 대학원에 진학했을 당시를 회고해 보면, 예상했던 바와 달리 전문적 학술 용어로 이루어지는 영어 수업을 따라가는 것보다 수업 외의 교수님이나 학교 친구들, 학교 밖에서의 원어민들과의 대화 등 대부분 실생활에서 이뤄지는 영어 실력을 향상시키는 것이 훨씬 더 어려웠다는 점이다. 그러다 커리큘럼 중 하나였던 Vocabulary 수업에서 이디엄에 관한 주제로 연구 리포트를 쓰고 발표했던 적이 있는데, 과제를 준비하는 동안 이디엄이 실제 영어의 구어체에서 꽤 많은 비중을 차지하고 있다는 것을 알게 되었다. 한 예로, 리얼리티 프로그램에 나온 배우가 "She gave me the cold shoulder."라는 말을 했는데, 처음엔 '왜 차가운 어깨를 주는 걸까?' 하고 의아한 생각을 했었다. 나중에 이 이디엄의 뜻이 '쌀쌀하게 대하다'라는 것을 알고 난 뒤에야 비로소 그 프로그램 속 내용에 관한 맥락을 이해할 수 있었다. 실제 이디엄 수업을 듣고 나서 많은 OTT 프로그램, TV 또는 영화 속 대화에 나오는 안 들렸던 이디엄이 들리기 시작하였고, 이디엄의 뜻을 알고 나서 예전엔 알아듣지 못했던 대화들을 점점 더 이해하게 되었을 때에는 많은 희열감을 느낄 수 있었다.

글쓴이가 체험했던 바를 학생들에게 전달해 주기 위해 유학을 마치고 학교로 복귀한 뒤 자유 학기 수업을 통해 이디엄 수업을 진행한 적이 있다. 그 당시 수업을 준비하고 진행하면서 아쉬웠던 점이 크게 두 가지 있었는데; 첫째, 대부분의 이디엄 교재들은 이디엄이 왜 그런 의미를 갖게 되었는지에 관한 유래에 대한 설명 없이 이디엄의 뜻만 소개하는 데 그쳤다는 것이고, 둘째, 이디엄을 좀 더 쉽게 익히기 위한 연상 이미지가 없어 인터넷을 통해 관련 이미지를 검색하고 제공하는 데 많은 어려움을 겪었다는 것이다. 따라서 글쓴이는 이디엄 수업을 통해 실제로 느꼈던 아쉬움을 채우고자 이디엄의 유래와 관련 이미지를 제공해 주는 교재를 만드는 데 집중하였다. 다만 미술 비전공자의 미미한 그림 실력에 대해서는 많은 양해 부탁드린다.

아무쪼록 이 교재가 Communicative English Proficiency를 향상시키고, 학습한 이디엄들을 활용하여 좀 더 컬러풀하고 풍요로운 의사소통의 기회를 갖는 데 미약하나마 도움이 되기를 바란다.

이 책을 쓰기까지 항상 힘이 되어주는 사랑하는 나의 가족, 나의 영어 조력자 John, 여러 조언을 아끼지 않아 준 BFF Sunny로부터의 많은 도움이 있었다. 마지막으로 항상 교사로서의 나의 롤 모델이자 영감 그 자체이신 나의 어머니께 특별한 감사를 표하고 싶다.

〈교재 활용을 위한 Tips〉

Step Ⅰ. 각 알파벳(A~Z)에 해당하는 단어를 포함한 이디엄 리스트를 보고 이미 내가 알고 있는 이디엄이 있는지 체크해 본다.
(♣ These are the List of Idioms A. Are there any idioms you already know? If not, try to guess the meaning of the idioms below.)

Step Ⅱ. 이디엄 관련 연상 이미지와 주어진 대화를 보고 이디엄이 어떤 의미를 가지고 있을지 추측해 본다.
(- Guess the meaning of the idiom in the dialogue below.)
☞ 이디엄 관련 이미지는 시각적으로 학습에 익숙한 Visual Learner들이 그림에서 연상되는 이미지를 통해 좀 더 쉽게 이디엄을 암기할 수 있게 하기 위함이다.

Step Ⅲ. 이디엄의 표면적 의미와 비유적 의미를 보며 자신이 추측했던 의미와 비교해 본다.
☞ 대부분의 이디엄의 표면적(literal) 의미와 비유적(figurative) 의미가 다르기 때문에 이디엄의 학습이 별도로 필요한 것이다.

Step Ⅳ. 이디엄 관련 유래(◐ History)를 통해 이디엄을 익히도록 한다.
☞ 이디엄의 유래를 정리하면서 대부분의 영어 어휘의 유래가 크게 1. 그리스 로마 신화, 2. 성경, 3. 셰익스피어 문학의 세 줄기로 나뉜다는 점을 알게 되었다. 이디엄 관련 유래의 학습은 영어라는 언어 능력 향상뿐만 아니라 영어 문화에 관한 배경 지식과 이해 또한 넓힐 수 있는 기회가 되리라고 생각한다.

Step V. 학습한 이디엄을 포함한 간단한 (일기)글이나 대화 글을 작성해 보며 복습한다. 또는 미드나 영화 등에서 학습한 이디엄이 사용되는지 집중하며 시청하거나, 친구들과 온오프라인 상에서 이디엄을 활용한 간단한 대화를 나눠 본다.
(♣ Make your own dialogue.)

☞ 교재를 읽는 수동적 학습(passive learning)에 그치는 것이 아니라 직접 써 보고 말하는 능동적 학습(active learning)을 한다면 영어 능력을 향상시키는 데 훨씬 효과가 클 것이다.

〈이 교재를 수업에 활용하실 영어 선생님들께〉

1. 이 교재는 정규 영어 수업 시간보다는 자유 학기 또는 창의적 체험 활동을 통한 수업에 활용하시는 것을 추천해 드린다.
2. 교사가 일방적으로 이디엄을 소개하며 가르치는 것보다 학생들에게 역할을 배분하여 일정 이디엄을 발표할 수 있는 기회를 주는 것도 좋다.
3. 이디엄의 비유적인 의미를 가르치기 전에 학생들에게 연상 이미지를 소개하며 비유적인 의미를 추측하도록 하는 것은 동기 유발에 도움이 될 수 있을 것이다.
4. 학기 수업이 끝날 때쯤에는 마음에 들었던 이디엄을 3~5개 정도 선택하게 하여 이디엄을 포함한 4컷 만화(짧은 동영상인 애니메이션 제작도 가능), 광고 카피를 이디엄으로 바꾸기, 짧은 상황극 발표하기 등의 다양한 활동을 통해 학생들이 자신이 학습한 것에 대한 결과물을 가짐으로써 성취감을 느낄 수 있는 기회를 제공하는 것도 좋을 듯싶다.

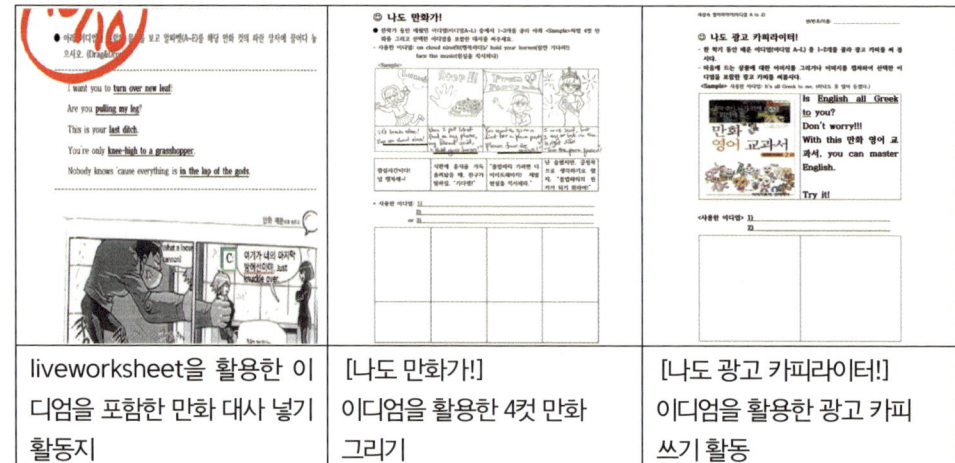

| liveworksheet을 활용한 이디엄을 포함한 만화 대사 넣기 활동지 | [나도 만화가!] 이디엄을 활용한 4컷 만화 그리기 | [나도 광고 카피라이터!] 이디엄을 활용한 광고 카피 쓰기 활동 |

Reference

dictionary of idioms and their origins(저자: Linda & Roger Flavell / 출판사: Kyle Cathie Limited 2006)

Idioms from A to Z: A

-A-

♣ These are the List of Idioms A. Are there any idioms you already know? If not, try to guess the meaning of the idioms below.

- taken **aback** -- ☐
- **above** board -- ☐
- **Achilles**' heel -- ☐
- **all** systems go -- ☐
- to write like an **angel** ------------------------------------ ☐
- in **apple-pie** order -- ☐
- tied to one's mother's **apron** strings ------------------ ☐
- to have an **axe** to grind ---------------------------------- ☐

⊙ taken **aback**

- Guess the meaning of the idiom in the dialogue below.

Suzie: I was completely _taken aback_ by your appetite at dinner. You ate four hamburgers in total.

Ben: Easy as pie for me.

L.M(표면적 의미)	F.M(비유적 의미)
뒤로 젖혀진	깜짝 놀라다(surprised, shocked)

- History: 배의 돛이 갑자기 부는 바람에 뒤로 젖혀지듯이, 갑작스러운 일에 대해서 뒤로 자빠질 듯이 놀란다는 의미로 쓰이게 됨.

♣ Make your own dialogue.

◎ above board

- Guess the meaning of the idiom in the dialogue below.

Suzie: Are you satisfied with the new deal?

Ben: Sort of. I guess it was **above board** at least.

L.M(표면적 의미)	F.M(비유적 의미)
테이블 위로	정직한(honest), 공명정대한

- History: 'board'는 'table'과 같은 의미로 쓰였는데, 테이블 아래는 가려져 있기 때문에 감추고 싶은 비밀스러운 의미가 있는 반대로, 테이블 위는 솔직하게 내놓는다는 의미.

♣ Make your own dialogue.

⊙ <mark>Achilles'</mark> heel

- Guess the meaning of the idiom in the dialogue below.

Suzie: Congrats on winning at the basketball match. How did you beat them?

Ben: Well, we had taller players than them. Their small height was kind of their _Achilles' heel_.

L.M(표면적 의미)	F.M(비유적 의미)
아킬레스건(발뒤꿈치)	누군가의 약점(a weak point in someone)

- History: 고대 그리스 신화에 따르면, 아킬레스의 엄마가 아킬레스가 단명한다는 이야기를 듣고 아들의 장수를 바라며 영원한 생명을 얻는다는 샘물에 아킬레스의 발목을 붙잡고 담갔는데, 정작 발뒤꿈치 부분만은 샘물에 닿지 않아 훗날 그 부분에 화살을 맞은 아킬레스가 죽었다고 함. 아킬레스건은 바로 그 신화에서 유래함.

♣ Make your own dialogue.

⊙ **all** systems go

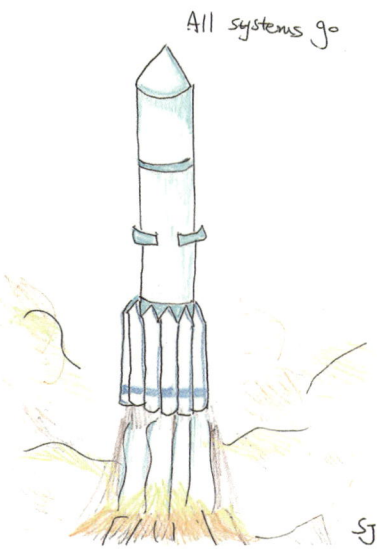

- Guess the meaning of the idiom in the dialogue below.

Suzie: Are you ready for the audition for the school play, *Romeo and Juliet*?
Ben: I'm a little nervous, but I guess it's *all systems go*.

L.M(표면적 의미)	F.M(비유적 의미)
모든 시스템이 잘 돌아간다	실행을 위한 만반의 준비가 된 (everything is ready for action)

- History: 우주선 발사가 성공하기 위해서는 아주 세세한 부분까지 완벽하게 시스템이 잘 돌아가야만 했음. 1960년대에 미국에서 우주선을 발사하는 것을 TV로 생중계했는데, 이때 우주선 발사를 위한 모든 것이 다 잘 돌아가고 있다, 즉 만반의 준비가 잘 되어 있다는 의미로 처음 사용되었음.

♣ Make your own dialogue.

Idioms from A to Z: A

⊙ to write like an angel

- Guess the meaning of the idiom in the dialogue below.

Suzie: I like the story of the movie, *Parasite*. It depicts a reality that our society is grappling with.

Ben: You can say that again. The write of the movie <u>writes like an *angel*</u>.

L.M(표면적 의미)	F.M(비유적 의미)
천사처럼 글을 쓰다	글쓰기에 천부적인 재능을 지닌; to be a gifted writer of poetry or prose)

- History: Angelo라는 사람의 아름다운 필체를 보고 유래되었으나, Angelo가 angel로 바뀌어 쓰이기 시작했고, 현재는 글쓰기에 천부적 재능이 있음을 비유적으로 표현하는 데 사용됨.

♣ Make your own dialogue.

◉ in apple-pie order

In apple pie order   SJ

- Guess the meaning of the idiom in the dialogue below.

Suzie: Your room is always in *apple*-pie order.

Ben: Thanks. I like tidying up my room.

L.M(표면적 의미)	F.M(비유적 의미)
애플파이가 질서정연하게 잘린	적절한 곳에 모든 것이 잘 정돈된; everything neatly arranged in its proper place

- History: 애플파이 위에 얹어진 사과가 정확한 사이즈로 잘 잘린 모습에서 유래되어 사용됨.

♣ Make your own dialogue.

Idioms from A to Z: A

◉ tied to one's mother's apron strings

− Guess the meaning of the idiom in the dialogue below.

Suzie: We missed you at the party last night. It was so much fun.

Ben: I know⋯. but I couldn't come because my mom wouldn't let me come to the party.

Suzie: Aren't you tied to your mother's *apron* strings?

Ben: NEVER! I am not a mommy's boy.

L.M(표면적 의미)	F.M(비유적 의미)
엄마의 앞치마 끝에 묶여 있는	엄마의 컨트롤 하에 엄격하게 관리되는 젊은 사람에게 일컬어지는; said of a young man who is kept strictly under his mother's control

− History: 앞치마는 보통 강인한 여성(엄마)을 상징하는 물건으로 사용되는데, 엄마의 앞치마 끈에 묶여 있는 의미에서 여자(보통 엄마)에게 꼼짝 못 하는 아들 또는 젊은 남자를 의미하는 것으로 사용됨.

♣ **Make your own dialogue.**

◉ to have an axe to grind

− Guess the meaning of the idiom in the dialogue below.

Suzie: I bought this for you. Here it is.

Ben: For what? Don't you have an axe to grind or something? Haha.

L.M(표면적 의미)	F.M(비유적 의미)
갈 도끼를 가지고 있는	비밀스러운 동기를 가지고 있는; to have a secret motive

− History: 1) 도끼날은 완벽하게 갈지 못한다는 한계를 받아들여서, 흠이 있지만 어쩔 수 없이 사용한다는 의미. 뭔가 밝힐 수 없지만, 비밀스러운 동기를 가지고 있다는 의미로 사용됨.

2) 벤자민 프랭클린의 이야기에 나오는 일화처럼, 완벽한 날을 가진 도끼를 갖고자 하는 젊은이에게 대장장이가 숫돌을 받는 조건으로 그렇게 갈아 주겠다고 제안한 점에서 무언가 조건을 받아들이는 데에는 숨은 동기가 있다는 의미로 사용됨.

♣ Make your own dialogue.

Idioms from A to Z: B

-B-

♣ These are the List of Idioms B. Are there any idioms you already know? If not, try to guess the meaning of the idioms below.

- to **bring** home the **bacon** ---------------------------- ☐
- **bag** and **baggage** ---------------------------------- ☐
- **baker**'s dozen -------------------------------------- ☐
- The **balloon** goes up --------------------------------- ☐
- to **bark** up the wrong tree ---------------------------- ☐
- jump on the **bandwagon** ------------------------------ ☐
- to spill the **beans** ----------------------------------- ☐
- to **beat** about(around) the **bush** --------------------- ☐
- **bee**'s knees --------------------------------------- ☐
- to **bite** the **bullet** ---------------------------------- ☐
- (like a bolt) from/out of the **blue** --------------------- ☐

⊙ to bring home the bacon

- Guess the meaning of the idiom in the dialogue below.

Suzie: Why the long face?

Ben: My dad got fired yesterday. Who's going to <u>*bring* home the *bacon*</u> from now on?

L.M(표면적 의미)	F.M(비유적 의미)
집에 베이컨을 가져오다	본인 또는 가족을 위해서 충분한 돈을 벌다; 뭔가에서 성공을 이루다; to earn enough to support oneself and one's family; to succeed in something

- History: 옛날 영국에서 모범적인 부부로 뽑힌 이들에게 상품으로 베이컨을 주는 문화가 있었는데, 이 대회에 뽑히기 위한 조건이 매우 까다로워서 상품이었던 베이컨을 얻는 것이 힘들었다는 데서 유래함.

♣ Make your own dialogue.

⊙ bag and baggage

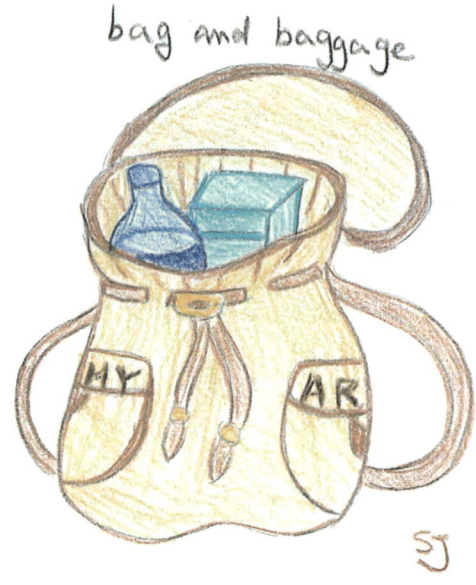

− Guess the meaning of the idiom in the dialogue below.

Suzie: I heard you were caught in a lie about playing games. What happened?

Ben: Mom was very upset and she threw me out onto the street, *bag and baggage.*

L.M(표면적 의미)	F.M(비유적 의미)
가방과 짐	모든 소지품(소유품)(with all one's possessions)

− History: 전쟁 시에 가방이나 짐(소지품)을 적군에게 빼앗기지 않고 잘 지킬 수 있도록 주의를 주었던 데에서 유래함.

♣ Make your own dialogue.

◉ baker's dozen

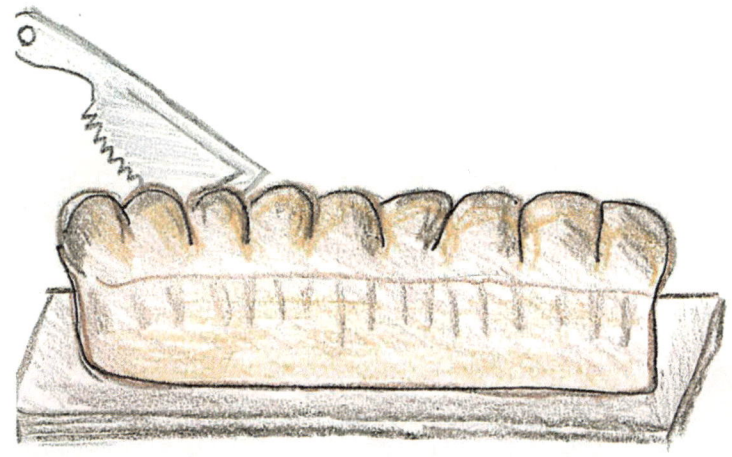

- Guess the meaning of the idiom in the dialogue below.

Suzie: I got a *baker's dozen* from that new bakery.

Ben: You're okay. Yeah, I heard that the owner of that bakery gives every 50th customers a *baker's dozen* on every Sunday.

L.M(표면적 의미)	F.M(비유적 의미)
제빵사의 12	12가 아닌 13개를 의미함 ;덤

- History: 베이커리 장사가 빵을 13조각으로 잘라 놓고도 12조각인 것처럼 팔면서 마치 남은 한 조각은 덤인 것처럼 얹어 주었던 데에서 유래함.

♣ Make your own dialogue.

⊙ The balloon goes up

- Guess the meaning of the idiom in the dialogue below.

Suzie: When does the party start?

Ben: The *balloon* goes up soon.

L.M(표면적 의미)	F.M(비유적 의미)
풍선이 위로 올라간다	문젯거리/유흥거리/행동이 막 시작되려 하는; the trouble/excitement/action is about to begin

- History: 전쟁 시에 어떤 작전을 개시할 때 풍선을 띄워서 시작 신호를 보냈다는 데에서 유래함.

♣ Make your own dialogue.

⊙ to bark up the wrong tree

- Guess the meaning of the idiom in the dialogue below.

Suzie: Did you eat my chocolate muffin? I had left it for dessert after lunch.
Ben: You're _barking_ up the wrong tree. Absolutely NO!!!
Suzie: Where is it, then?

L.M(표면적 의미)	F.M(비유적 의미)
엉뚱한 나무를 올려다보며 짖는다	to follow a wrong line of enquiry; 잘못 짚다, 엉뚱한 사람을 비난하다

- History: 야행성 동물인 너구리(racoon)을 사냥하기 위해서 사냥개들이 너구리가 올라가 있는 나무를 쳐다보고 사냥꾼이 올 때까지 짖어댔는데, 시력이 좋지 않은 개들이 밤이 되면 종종 다른 엉뚱한 나무를 쳐다보며 짖었다는 데에서 유래함.

♣ Make your own dialogue.

◉ jump on the bandwagon

- Guess the meaning of the idiom in the dialogue below.

Suzie: Climate change is an important issue in our society.

Ben: Yeah, most politicians are eager to <u>jump on the</u> environmental <u>*bandwagon*,</u> too.

L.M(표면적 의미)	F.M(비유적 의미)
서커스 마차(bandwagon)에 올라타다; (많은 사람들이 함께하는) 행사에 가다	우세한 편에 서다; 시류에 편승하다; to support a cause that looks as if it will succeed, often for personal profit or advantage

- History: 미국에서 서커스가 동네를 지날 때마다 사람들이 서커스 마차 위에 올라타서 정치적 선전을 했던 데에서 유래함.

♣ Make your own dialogue.

Idioms from A to Z: B

⊙ to spill the beans

To spill the beans

- Guess the meaning of the idiom in the dialogue below.

Suzie: Wasn't the surprise party for Sam supposed to be a secret?
Ben: I wonder who spilled the *beans*.

L.M(표면적 의미)	F.M(비유적 의미)
콩이 자루에서 흘러나오다	to let out a secret; 비밀이 밝혀지다/새어 나오다

- History: 'spill'은 누설하다/'beans'은 know the beans에서 유래하여 정보/지식을 알고 있다는 표현에서 사용되어 '정보/지식'을 뜻함. 이처럼 콩들이 자루에서 바깥으로 흘러나오듯이 지식이나 정보가 세상에 알려진다는 의미로 쓰임.

♣ Make your own dialogue.

⊙ to beat about(around) the bush

To beat around the bush SJ

- Guess the meaning of the idiom in the dialogue below.

Ben: Suzie, I like your sneakers. They are so cute, and you look so handsome today.

Suzie: Don't *beat* around the *bush*. Just tell me what you want from me.

Ben: Actually….

L.M(표면적 의미)	F.M(비유적 의미)
덤불 숲 주변을 (몽둥이로) 치다	to go about something in a roundabout way 돌려서 말하다/변죽을 울리다

- History: 사냥을 하기 전에, 겁주기 위해서 주변의 덤불을 몽둥이로 쳤던 것에 유래함.

♣ Make your own dialogue.

Idioms from A to Z: B

⊙ bee's knees

- Guess the meaning of the idiom in the dialogue below.

Suzie: Did you see William dancing on the stage at the school festival?
Ben: Yes. He's a great dancer. He thinks he is the <u>*bee's knees*</u>, too.

L.M(표면적 의미)	F.M(비유적 의미)
벌의 무릎	the best 최고의

- History: 1920년대에 유행한 말로, 동물들에게 존재하지 않는 신체 부위를 가리켜서 '최상'의 의미를 표현함.

♣ Make your own dialogue.

⊙ to bite the bullet

- Guess the meaning of the idiom in the dialogue below.

Suzie: The due date for the final project is approaching.

Ben: I know it's a hard work, but you have to *bite the bullet* and do it.

L.M(표면적 의미)	F.M(비유적 의미)
총알을 깨물다	to fact up to a difficult situation; to screw up one's courage; 어렵거나 불쾌한 상황에 맞닥뜨리다

- History: 전쟁 시에 한 손에는 총을, 다른 한 손에는 화약을 가지고 있어서, 총에 장전을 할 때 입으로 탄약 끝의 종이 포장을 뜯어낸다는 데에서 유래함.

♣ Make your own dialogue.

⊙ (like a bolt) from/out of the blue

from/ out of the blue

- Guess the meaning of the idiom in the dialogue below.

Suzie: The movie was so thrilling, right?
Ben: Yes. When the ghost appeared <u>out of the *blue*</u>, I screamed.
Suzie: So did I.

L.M(표면적 의미)	F.M(비유적 의미)
파란 하늘에서	totally unexpected, suddenly; 갑작스러운, 기대치 못한 상황

- History: 'blue'는 파란 하늘을 뜻하는데, 갑자기 파란/맑은 하늘에 번개가 친다는 데에서 유래함. 'like a bolt'를 생략하고 나머지만 쓰이는 경우도 많음.

♣ Make your own dialogue.

Idioms from A to Z: C

-C-

♣ These are the List of Idioms C. Are there any idioms you already know? If not, try to guess the meaning of the idioms below.

- ⊙ take the **cake** -- ☐
- ⊙ burn the **candle** at both ends ------------------------- ☐
- ⊙ not to hold a **candle** to someone / something ------------ ☐
- ⊙ (blood) on the **carpet** ---------------------------------- ☐
- ⊙ put the **cart** before the horse ------------------------ ☐
- ⊙ on **cloud** nine --- ☐
- ⊙ a **catch** 22 (situation) -------------------------------- ☐
- ⊙ get/have **cold** feet ------------------------------------ ☐
- ⊙ go **cold** turkey -- ☐
- ⊙ give someone the **cold** shoulder ---------------------- ☐
- ⊙ **couch** potato --- ☐

⊙ take the cake

To take the cake   SJ

- Guess the meaning of the idiom in the dialogue below.

Suzie: BTS takes the cake for both singing and dancing.
Ben: You can say that again!

L.M(표면적 의미)	F.M(비유적 의미)
케이크를 가져가다	특출 난; 탁월한; ₩to deserve honour or merit; to be outrageous

- History: 19세기 미국 남부 농장에서는 흑인 노예들이 2박자로 된 'cakewalk'라는 춤을 즐겨 추었는데, 그 춤에서 우승한 커플에게는 상품으로 케이크가 주어졌다는 데에서 유래함.

♣ Make your own dialogue.

◉ burn the candle at both ends

- Guess the meaning of the idiom in the dialogue below.

Suzie: Will aced the final term again. He is such an energizer.
Ben: Yeah, he burns the *candle* at both ends when it comes to studying.

L.M(표면적 의미)	F.M(비유적 의미)
초의 양 끝을 태우다	(에너지를 소진할 정도로) 밤새 열심히 놀거나 공부하다; to work or play until late into the night and then get up early next morning to invest energy

- History: 초의 양쪽 심지가 타들어 갈 정도로 '뭔가에 집중하여 열심히 한다'는 의미에서 유래함.

♣ Make your own dialogue.

◉ not to hold a candle to someone / something

- Guess the meaning of the idiom in the dialogue below.
Suzie: I went to the Pavarotti's concert last night. It was so amazing.
Ben: Yeah, I guess so. Any other singers can't hold a *candle* to Pavarotti.

L.M(표면적 의미)	F.M(비유적 의미)
~에(게) 초를 들지 않다	열등한; 잘하지 못하는; 하찮은; to be inferior to; not do as well as

- History: 전기가 발명되기 전이었던 16세기에는 해가 지고 어두워진 이후에는, 일할 때 초를 밝혀야 했었는데, 그러기 위해서는 일할 때 누군가 옆에서 촛불을 들어서 도와주고 했다고 함. 보통 그런 일은 하인이나 조수와 같은 낮은 신분의 사람들이 했었기 때문에, 많은 기술이 필요하지 않은, 즉 하찮은 일이라는 뜻에서 '어떤 일을 잘하지 못한다'라는 의미가 되어 사용되었다고 함.

♣ **Make your own dialogue.**

◉ (blood) on the carpet

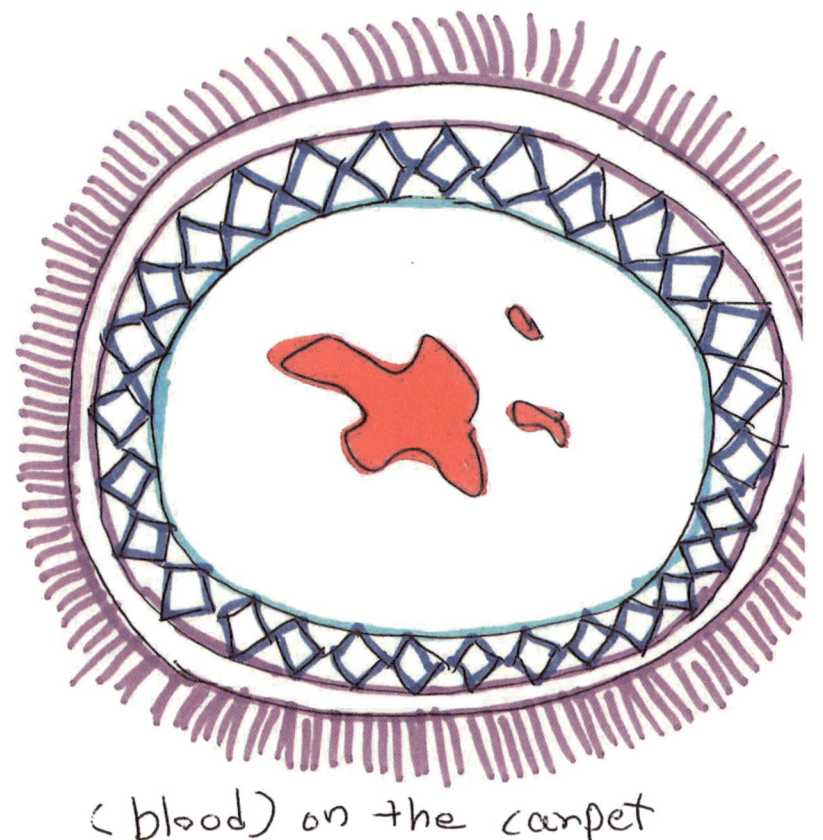

- Guess the meaning of the idiom in the dialogue below.

Suzie: Are you done cleaning the English room?

Ben: Oh, I forgot to do.

Suzie: You'd better hurry to finish it before the teacher comes back. Otherwise there will be <u>blood on the *carpet*.</u>

L.M(표면적 의미)	F.M(비유적 의미)
카펫 위의 피	심한 질책(꾸중); 대량 실업; a stern rebuke; strong action; widespread job loss

- History: 카펫은 수십 세기 전에는 터키라는 나라에서부터만 수입되었던 아주 고급스러운 물건으로, 카펫은 부자들의 집에서만 소유되어 '부'의 상징이었다고 함. 보통 시종 등을 꾸짖을 때 카펫 위에 세웠으며, 시종들이 카펫 위에 서 있을 때는 주인들에게 호되게 혼이 나는 경우가 대부분이었다는 데서 유래함.

♣ Make your own dialogue.

◉ put the cart before the horse

- Guess the meaning of the idiom in the dialogue below.

Suzie: I feel like there is something wrong in our group project.
Ben: We seem to put the *cart* before the horse.
　　　We need to work systematically.

L.M(표면적 의미)	F.M(비유적 의미)
말 앞에 마차를 두다	본말전도; 일의 앞뒤 순서가 잘못되다; to reverse the sensible order, to do something back to front

- History: 마차를 끌기 위해서는 말이 마차 앞에 위치하여 끌어야 하는데, 말의 앞에 마차를 두었다는 데에서 유래하여 사용됨.

♣ Make your own dialogue.

◉ on cloud nine

- Guess the meaning of the idiom in the dialogue below.

Suzie: William finally asked me out.
Ben: Wow, you must be <u>on *cloud* nine</u>.

L.M(표면적 의미)	F.M(비유적 의미)
아홉 번째 구름 위에	최상으로 행복한(supremely happy)

- History: 행복한 감정을 느낄 때 마치 구름 위에 떠다니는 모습이 상상되는 것에서 유래함. 또한 구름을 단계별로 나눌 때 가장 높은 위치에 있는 구름에 해당하는 것을 적란운이라 하는데, 그 구름이 'level 9'으로 불리게 된 데에서 행복의 수치가 가장 높은 구름 위에 있는 것처럼 최고조의 상태라는 것을 뜻하게 되었다고도 함.

♣ Make your own dialogue.

◉ a catch 22 (situation)

- Guess the meaning of the idiom in the dialogue below.

Suzie: I guess I'm in a <u>Catch-22 (situation)</u>. I need to get Covid-19 vaccination, but I'm also worried about its side-effects.

Ben: Which one has more pluses for you?

L.M(표면적 의미)	F.M(비유적 의미)
22번째 복무 사항	진퇴양난; 딜레마(a troublesome situation from which there is no apparent escape since the solution leads back to the original difficulty)

- History: 미국 소설가인 Joseph Heller가 쓴 Catch-22에서 유래한 이디엄임. 공군들이 따라야 할 복무 사항(catch) 중에서 22번째에 해당하는 지침의 내용이, 훈련에 나가지 않으려면 직접 정신 상태가 정상이 아닌, 즉 자신이 미쳤다는 것을 증명해야 하는데, 훈련에 나가는 일과 자신이 미치지 않았다는 일을 증명하는 일, 둘 중 하나를 선택해야 하는 해결책이 보이지 않는 상황을 뜻하는 데에서 유래함. 선택에는 항상 두 가지 조건이 따르기 때문에 2라는 순서를 두 번 쓴 점도 이러한 뜻에 영향을 주었다고 함.

♣ **Make your own dialogue.**

Idioms from A to Z: C

⊙ get/have cold feet

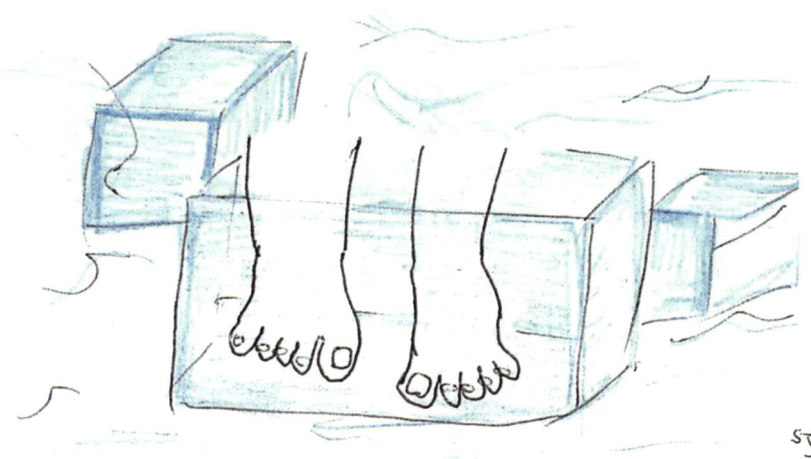

- Guess the meaning of the idiom in the dialogue below.

Suzie: How did the audition go for the school play?
Ben: I *got cold feet* right before my turn.

L.M(표면적 의미)	F.M(비유적 의미)
차가운 발을 갖다	긴장한(to feel anxious)

- History: 독일의 소설에 나오는 내용 중 카드 플레이어가 게임에서 빠져 나오고 싶은 핑곗거리를 찾다가 자신의 발이 너무 차갑기 때문에 게임을 더 이상 할 수 없어 그만두겠다고 말한 데에서 유래함. 게임이 잘 풀리지 않는 긴장된 감정을 나타내는 데 영향을 받음.

♣ Make your own dialogue.

◎ go cold turkey

- Guess the meaning of the idiom in the dialogue below.

Suzie: You played mobile games for five hours in a row. Can't you just stop playing?

Ben: I can't *go cold* turkey.

L.M(표면적 의미)	F.M(비유적 의미)
차가운 칠면조가 되다	약 등을 갑자기 끊어 버리다(to come off drugs abruptly); 하던 일을 갑자기 멈추다/그만두다

- History: 약물 치료를 받던 약물 중독자가 급작스럽게 약물을 끊어 버리면 피부가 마치 털이 뽑힌 칠면조처럼 울퉁불퉁한 거친 상태처럼 되는 데에서 유래함.

♣ Make your own dialogue.

◉ give someone the cold shoulder

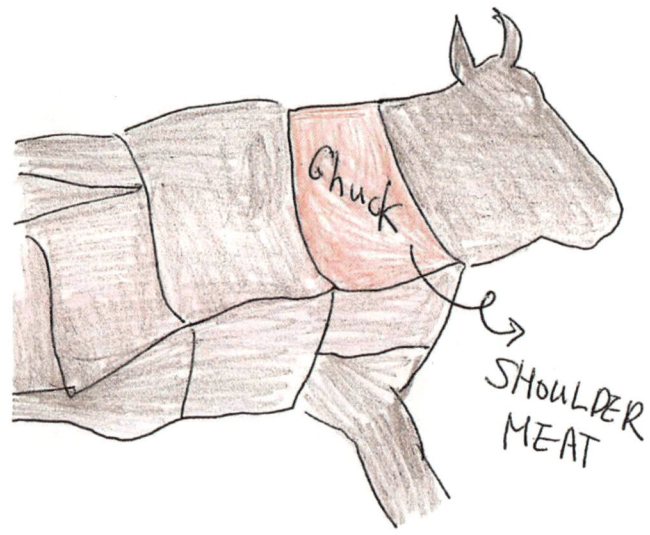

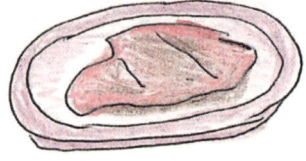

- Guess the meaning of the idiom in the dialogue below.

Suzie: Crystal <u>gave me the **cold** shoulder</u> at the party last night. I don't know what I did wrong to her.

Ben: Do you want me to ask Crystal for you?

L.M(표면적 의미)	F.M(비유적 의미)
누군가에게 차가운 어깨살 부위의 고기를 주다	누군가를 일부러 차갑게 대하다; to treat someone with intentional coldness

- History: 파티에 초대하여 손님들에게 음식을 대접할 때, 귀중한 손님의 순서대로 맛있는 고기 부위를 잘라서 대접하였다고 함. 반갑지 않은 손님이나 질척거리며 늦게까지 머무는 손님은 결국 마지막까지 남은 식은 고기(잘 안 나가는 어깨살 부위의 고기)를 받았다는 의미에서 유래함.

♣ Make your own dialogue.

Idioms from A to Z: C

⊙ couch potato

- Guess the meaning of the idiom in the dialogue below.

Suzie: Stop binge-watching TV! Get off from the sofa.
Ben: I have to finish watching *Squid Game* today. Come on!
Suzie: Seems like you're becoming a real **couch potato**.

L.M(표면적 의미)	F.M(비유적 의미)
의자(소파) 감자	무기력한 TV 중독자; some living a mindless life with minimum effort, an inactive TV addict

- History: 소파에 앉아서 하루 종일 TV를 보며 먹고 자고를 반복하는 무기력한 사람에서 연상된 표현. 이런 게으른 생활로 인해 감자의 형태처럼 배가 나오고 뚱뚱해진 이미지를 연관시킨 데에서 유래함.

♣ Make your own dialogue.

Idioms from A to Z: D

-D-

♣ These are the List of Idioms D. Are there any idioms you already know? If not, try to guess the meaning of the idioms below.

- a **dark** horse ---------------------------------- ☐
- **day** of reckoning ------------------------------ ☐
- **deaf** as a post -------------------------------- ☐
- talk/speak of the **devil** ----------------------- ☐
- a **die**-hard ------------------------------------ ☐
- in the **doghouse** ------------------------------- ☐
- to see a man about a **dog** ---------------------- ☐
- a lame **duck** ----------------------------------- ☐
- **double Dutch** ---------------------------------- ☐
- go **Dutch** -------------------------------------- ☐

◉ a dark horse

- Guess the meaning of the idiom in the dialogue below.

Suzie: I think Jimin will be the next school president.
Ben: Nobody knows yet. I heard recently Jung-guk is emerging as a dark horse.

L.M(표면적 의미)	F.M(비유적 의미)
어두운 색의 말	능력이 아직 알려지지 않거나 검증(시험)되지 않은 사람; a person whose abilities are not yet known and tested

- History: Benjamin Disraeli의 소설인 *The Young Duke*에서 처음으로 언급되었음. 경마에서 사람들에게 가장 애호를 받던 두 마리의 말들이 전혀 생각지도 않고 명단에서도 주목받지 못했던 어두운 색의 말에게 승리를 내어준 것에서 유래함. 현재는 정치에서 사람들에게 기대를 받지 못했고 잘 알려지지 않았지만, 선두를 이끄는 정치 후보자를 가리키는 말로 사용됨.

♣ Make your own dialogue.

⊙ day of reckoning

- Guess the meaning of the idiom in the dialogue below.

Suzie: I'm nervous 'cause the <u>day of reckoning</u> for the project is almost upon me.

Ben: No need to worry. I know you did your best. I wish you a good luck.

L.M(표면적 의미)	F.M(비유적 의미)
심판의 날	심판의 날(시간) (a time of giving a (final) account for one's actions; a time when one's success or failure in an endeavour will be made known)

- History: 성경에 나오는 글귀로, 예수님이 부활하셔서 산 자와 죽은 자를 심판하러 오실 거라고 선언한 데에서 유래함.

♣ Make your own dialogue.

◉ deaf as a post

- Guess the meaning of the idiom in the dialogue below.

Suzie: My parents are _deaf as a post_ when it comes to getting a tattoo.
Ben: Mine as well.

L.M(표면적 의미)	F.M(비유적 의미)
문설주처럼 못 듣는	완전히 귀먹은; 들을 수 없는(totally deaf)

- History: 성경 말씀 중에는 비유적인 표현이 많이 사용되었는데 이 표현은 비유 중 직유적인 표현으로 '귀먹음'은 무생물의 물건에 많이 비유되어 쓰였는데 post(문설주)도 그중 하나의 예로 사용되었음.

♣ Make your own dialogue.

⊙ talk/speak of the devil

- Guess the meaning of the idiom in the dialogue below.

Suzie: Did you hear that Ben was dumped by his girlfriend again?

Ben: **_Speak of the devil_**···, he is coming.

L.M(표면적 의미)	F.M(비유적 의미)
악마에 대해 말하다	호랑이도 제 말 하면 온다 (누군가에 대해서 말하면 그 사람이 갑자기 나타난다)

- History: devil(악마)는 악마의 이름을 거론했을 때만 소환이 되는데, 악마의 이름을 거론하면 어디선가 갑자기 나타난다는 의미에서 유래함.

♣ Make your own dialogue.

⊙ a die-hard

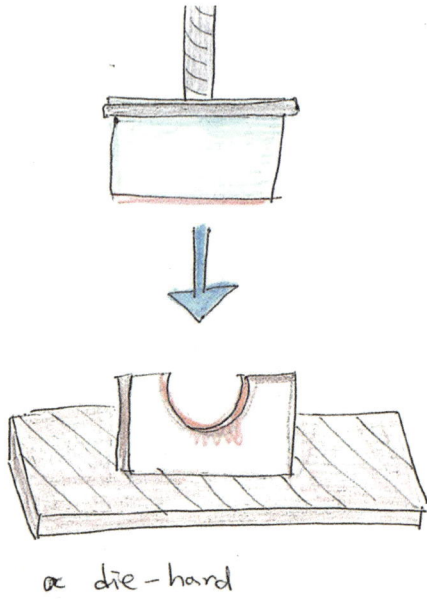

a die-hard

– Guess the meaning of the idiom in the dialogue below.
Suzie: My dad votes for a candidate depending on the party. It doesn't matter whether or not a candidate is good enough.
Ben: Mine, too. He is a *die-hard* as yours.

L.M(표면적 의미)	F.M(비유적 의미)
죽기 힘든 사람	정치적 변화를 거부하는 보수적이거나 완고한 사람

– History: 1784년 *The Gentleman's Magazine*에 쓰였던 신조어로, 런던의 Tyburn에 있었던 교수대에 어떤 범죄자가 끝까지 죽기를 거부하며 힘들게 죽었다는 의미에서 유래함. 20세기에 와서 변화를 거부하고 싫어하는 정치적 파벌(파당)을 의미하게 됨.

♣ **Make your own dialogue.**

◉ in the doghouse

- Guess the meaning of the idiom in the dialogue below.

Ben: I am *in the doghouse* with my girlfriend.
Suzie: Again? What did you do this time?

L.M(표면적 의미)	F.M(비유적 의미)
개집 안에서	in disgrace 불명예스럽게; 인기가 없는; 사이가 서먹해진

- History: 나쁜 개는 집 밖으로 내쫓아지고 처벌로써 개집 안에 갇혀 지내게 되었던 데에서 유래함.

♣ Make your own dialogue.

◉ to see a man about a dog

– Guess the meaning of the idiom in the dialogue below.

Suzie: This party is too boring.

Ben: How about sneaking out saying we need to *see a man about a dog*?

L.M(표면적 의미)	F.M(비유적 의미)
개에 관해 이야기하기 위해 사람을 만나다	a phrase used to disguise the purpose of one's business; 원래의 목적을 숨기기 위해서 사용되는 문구; "화장실 다녀올게"

– History: 연극 *Flying Scud*라는 멜로드라마 연극에 나온 대사로, 곤란한 상황에서 빠져나오기 위해서 핑계를 대는 데 쓰였음. 예를 들면, 술이 금지되었던 시기에 술을 사러 간다는 얘기를 못하고 화장실에 다녀오겠고 말하는 것처럼, 원래의 목적을 말하지 못하고 다른 핑계를 대는 것. '개'는 애완동물로 흔한 소재였고, 현재 이 이디엄은 '화장실에 다녀올게'라는 의미로 많이 쓰이고 있음.

♣ Make your own dialogue.

Idioms from A to Z: D

⊙ a lame duck

– Guess the meaning of the idiom in the dialogue below.

Suzie: Our president is still very popular among the people.

Ben: You can say that again! His approval rate is close to 50%. I guess he is the first president that is not a lame duck in our history.

L.M(표면적 의미)	F.M(비유적 의미)
절뚝거리는(변변찮은) 오리	an ineffectual person; a failing business 무능력한 사람; 실패한 사업

– History: 18세기에 미국의 증권 거래소에서 동물을 빗대어서 쓰였던 속어로, 'bull'은 증시가 오르다, 'bear'는 증시가 떨어지다, 'lame duck'은 재정적인 약속을 지키지 못하는 브로커를 의미하는 것으로 사용됨. 미국의 남북 전쟁 이후로는 임기가 거의 끝날 즈음에 힘이 빠지거나 쇠해가는 정치인을 의미하는 것으로 사용됨.

♣ Make your own dialogue.

⊙ double Dutch

- Guess the meaning of the idiom in the dialogue below.

Suzie: Did you understand the online lecture on the metaverse?

Ben: No, it was **double Dutch** to me.

L.M(표면적 의미)	F.M(비유적 의미)
이중 네덜란드 언어	gibberish; incomprehensible speech; a language that one does not understand; 횡설수설; 이해할 수 없는 언어

- History: 누군가에게 모욕을 주고 싶을 때는 그 사람의 언어를 깔보는 데에서 유래하였는데, 영국인들에게 네덜란드가 강한 경제적 라이벌이었던 시절, 네덜란드인(Dutch)에게 모욕을 주고 싶어서 그들의 언어가 우스꽝스럽고 그저 횡설수설에 불과하다고 비꼬아 말한 데에서 유래함.

♣ Make your own dialogue.

◉ go Dutch

- Guess the meaning of the idiom in the dialogue below.

Suzie: Total is $30. Let's *go Dutch!*

Ben: No, this lunch is on me.

L.M(표면적 의미)	F.M(비유적 의미)
네덜란드식으로 가자!	to share the costs of an outing instead of allowing one's companion to pay; 지불할 때 각자 부담하다(특히 여성과의 데이트에서)

- History: 네덜란드에서 온 미국 이민자들이 특히 금전 관계에 있어서 신중한 면을 나타낸 데에서 유래하였음.

♣ Make your own dialogue.

Idioms from A to Z: E

-E-

♣ These are the List of Idioms E. Are there any idioms you already know? If not, try to guess the meaning of the idioms below.

- ⊙ to go in one **ear** and out the other ☐
- ⊙ an **eager** beaver ☐
- ⊙ to have/keep one's **ear(s)** to the ground ☐
- ⊙ My **ears** are burning. ☐
- ⊙ to **eat** someone out of house and home ☐
- ⊙ a bad/good **egg** ☐
- ⊙ to teach one's grandmother to suck **eggs** ☐
- ⊙ in/out of one's **element** ☐
- ⊙ to give one's **eye teeth** for something ☐

◉ to go in one *ear* and out the other

- Guess the meaning of the idiom in the dialogue below.

Suzie: You missed the important meeting today.

Ben: Oh my gosh! I totally forgot.

Suzie: Don't let it go in one *ear* and out the other!

L.M(표면적 의미)	F.M(비유적 의미)
한 귀로 가서 다른 쪽으로 나오다	to be heard but disregarded or easily forgotten; 한쪽 귀로 듣고 다른 쪽 귀로 나가다/쉽게 잊히는

- History: 정보가 뇌에 연관되어 처리되지 않은 채 머리를 그냥 통과하여 나간다는 오래된 개념에서 유래함.

♣ Make your own dialogue.

◎ an eager beaver

− Guess the meaning of the idiom in the dialogue below.

Suzie: I heard William aced the Engish test. He is such a genius.

Ben: I think he is also <u>an *eager* beaver.</u>

L.M(표면적 의미)	F.M(비유적 의미)
열성적인 비버	an overly zealous person, one who tries to impress others with enthusiasm and hard work; 모든 일에 열성인 사람/일(공부) 벌레

− History: 미국에서 'work like a beaver'라는 표현이 쓰일 정도로 beaver는 모든 일에 열성인 사람을 빗대어 쓰였는데, 특히 2차 세계 대전 동안 모든 영역에 열심히 지원해서 격렬하게 활동하는 사람을 일컬어 사용되었음. 'eager beaver'라는 두 단어를 함께 씀으로써 rhyme을 맞춤.

♣ Make your own dialogue.

⊙ to have/keep one's ear(s) to the ground

– Guess the meaning of the idiom in the dialogue below.

Suzie: Look at you. I love your big backpack.

Ben: Thanks. It is a trendy item nowadays.

Suzie: You always keep your *ears* to the ground.

L.M(표면적 의미)	F.M(비유적 의미)
땅바닥에 귀를 대고 있다	to listen carefully to current rumours and concerns, or to trends in public opinion; 귀를 기울이다(최근 일어나는 트렌드, 루머, 염려 등에)

– History: 인디언과 카우보이가 나오는 오래된 영화에서 흔하게 보이던 미국의 원주민 정찰병들이 귀를 땅에 대고 말이 접근해 오는 소리를 듣는 장면에서 유래함. 현재는 정치, 쇼 비즈니스, 패션업계에서 최근의 이벤트에 최선봉에 있어서 중요하게 여긴다는 의미로 많이 쓰임.

♣ **Make your own dialogue.**

◎ **My ears are burning.**

− Guess the meaning of the idiom in the dialogue below.

Suzie: My *ears* are burning.

Ben: That's a sign that someone is talking about you now.

L.M(표면적 의미)	F.M(비유적 의미)
귀가 화끈거린다(타고 있다)	a remark made by those who think they are being talked about; (누군가 내 얘기를 하는지) 귀가 간질거리는 증상 'burning' 대신에 'tingling'도 많이 쓰이기도 함

− History: 귀 부위가 간지럽거나 달아오르는 감각은 다른 누군가가 내 얘기를 하는 것으로 여겨짐. 고대 로마 시대부터 이러한 믿음이 시작되었는데, 오른쪽 귀가 달아오르면 누군가가 내 칭찬을 하고 있다고 여기고, 왼쪽 귀가 달아오르면 나쁜 의도로 인해 이야기를 듣는 것으로 여겼다고 함.

♣ Make your own dialogue.

⊙ to eat someone out of house and home

- Guess the meaning of the idiom in the dialogue below.

Suzie: Sam has a huge appetite.

Ben: Why are you saying so?

Suzie: He visited me yesterday. He <u>*ate* us out of house and home</u>.

L.M(표면적 의미)	F.M(비유적 의미)
어떤 사람의 집의 음식을 먹어 치우다	to consume a great deal and use up a person's resources; 엄청나게 소비하고 어떤 이의 자원(재원)을 탕진해 버리다

- History: 셰익스피어의 극본 중 하나인 *Henry* 4세의 2막에 나오는 Quickly라는 미망인이 자신에게 끊임없이 구애해 오는 Falstaff를 잡아서 가둬 달라고 불만을 토로하는 장면의 대사에서 유래한 표현임. 극 중에서 Falstaff가 빚을 탕진하고 사기를 친 점에 대해 그를 체포해 달라고 요청함.

♣ Make your own dialogue.

⊙ a bad/good egg

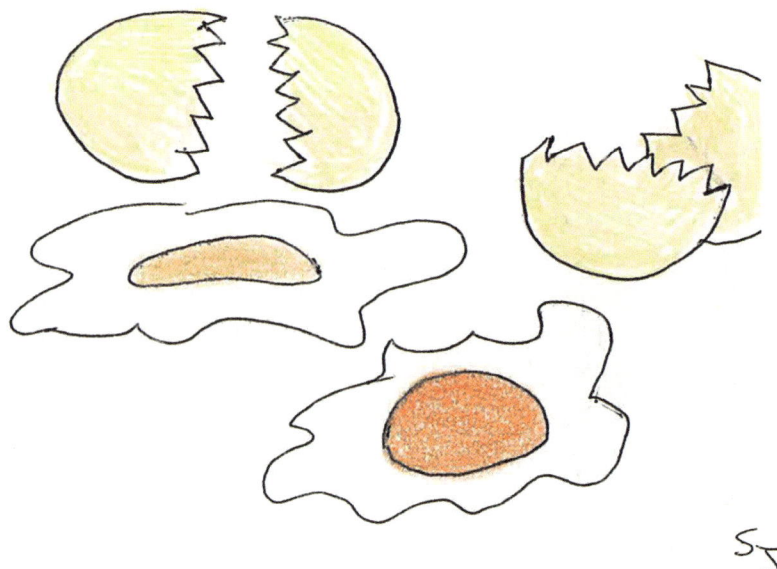

- Guess the meaning of the idiom in the dialogue below.

Suzie: I decided to break up with William.

Ben: Why? What happened?

Suzie: I don't think he is a good egg.

L.M(표면적 의미)	F.M(비유적 의미)
나쁜/좋은 달걀	a bad egg; an untrustworthy person /신뢰할 수 없는 사람 a good egg; dependable person /기댈 수 있는 사람

- History: 단지 달걀 껍데기를 외관으로 보는 것만으로는 달걀이 신선한지 아닌지를 판단할 수 없고, 달걀을 깨 보고서야 비로소 노른자가 중앙에 또렷이 모여 있는 것을 보고 신선한 달걀이란 것을 알 수 있듯이, 사람에 대해서도 겉만 보고 판단할 수 없고 시간이 지나 그 사람에 대해서 좀 더 잘 알게 되었을 때 판단이 가능하다는 데에서 유래함.

♣ Make your own dialogue.

⊙ to teach one's grandmother to suck eggs

− Guess the meaning of the idiom in the dialogue below.

Suzie: I will teach you how to play a chess.

Ben: Stop teaching your grandmother to suck eggs. I have played a chess way longer than you.

L.M(표면적 의미)	F.M(비유적 의미)
할머니께 달걀을 빨아 먹는 방법을 가르치다	to offer unnecessary advice to someone who is older and more experienced; 나이가 더 많거나 경험이 더 많은 사람에게 불필요한 충고를 제안하다

− History: 18세기부터 사용되었던 말로, 경험이 부족하면서도 자신보다 더 현명하고 나이 든 사람을 가르쳐야 한다고 생각하는 젊은 사람을 질책하기 위해서 쓰였음. 날달걀을 빨아먹는 것은 할머니의 연륜으로는 충분히 잘 알고 있음에도 불구하고 가르친다는 비꼼의 의미가 내포되어 있음.

♣ Make your own dialogue.

⊙ in/out of one's element

- Guess the meaning of the idiom in the dialogue below.

Suzie: How is your new job?
Ben: It is <u>in my *element*.</u> As you know, I enjoy taking photos.

L.M(표면적 의미)	F.M(비유적 의미)
구성 요소 안에/밖에 있는	at ease(쉬운, 마음이 편한) <-> ill at ease(마음이 불편한, 어색한)/본래의 활동 영역 안에 있는

- History: Earth(땅), water(물), air(공기), and fire(불)은 세상을 구성하는 4가지의 주요한 원소로 여겨졌는데, 각각의 기질에 빗대어 사람의 성격을 구분했던 데에서 유래함. 특히 4가지의 요소가 잘 어우러져 조화를 이루는 사람이냐 아니냐에 관한 것이 셰익스피어의 연극에서도 많이 인용되었음.

♣ Make your own dialogue.

⦿ to give one's eye teeth for something

- Guess the meaning of the idiom in the dialogue below.

Suzie: Can I borrow your new bike this Saturday? I will give my *eye teeth* for it.
Ben: I'm afraid I can't. I also need it on that day.

L.M(표면적 의미)	F.M(비유적 의미)
뭔가를 위해서 송곳니를 내주다	(to be willing) to make a great sacrifice to obtain something; 원하는 것을 얻기 위해서 무엇이든지 내놓는다

- History: 예로부터 eye teeth(송곳니)는 소중한 것으로 여겨졌는데, 송곳니가 나면 전체 치아가 다 갖춰져서 어른과 같은 지혜를 가지게 되었다고 여겨졌음.

♣ Make your own dialogue.

Idioms from A to Z: F

-F-

♣ These are the List of Idioms F. Are there any idioms you already know? If not, try to guess the meaning of the idioms below.

- the **face** that launched a thousand ships ☐
- to lose/save **face** ☐
- **fair** and square ☐
- a **fat** cat ☐
- to kill the **fatted** calf ☐
- a **feather** in one's cap ☐
- as **fit** as a **fiddle** ☐
- **feet** of clay ☐
- to have a **finger** in every pie ☐
- to be all **fingers** and thumbs ☐

- a drink like a **fish** (to drink like a **fish**) ──────────── ☐
- the **flavour** of the month ──────────────── ☐
- to **fly** off the handle ───────────────── ☐
- to take **French** leave ───────────────── ☐

⊙ the face that launched a thousand ships

- Guess the meaning of the idiom in the dialogue below.

Suzie: How was your blind date yesterday?

Ben: She is gorgeous. She has <u>the *face* that launched a thousand ships.</u>

L.M(표면적 의미)	F.M(비유적 의미)
천여 척의 배를 출항시킨 얼굴	a very beautiful woman; 아주 아름다운 여성

- History: Chirstopher Marlowe의 연극인 *The Tragical History of Doctor Faustus*(파우스트 박사의 비극적 역사)라는 연극의 한 대사에서 Helen 왕세자빈을 언급한 데에서 유래함. 트로이의 Paris 왕자가 그리스의 Menelaus 왕의 아름다운 부인인 Helen을 트로이로 납치해 왔던 것이 트로이 전쟁을 초래했던 데에서 유래함. 그리스 연합군은 트로이로 쳐들어가기 위해서 수천여 척의 배를 출항시켰다고 함.

♣ Make your own dialogue.

⊙ to lose/save **face**

- Guess the meaning of the idiom in the dialogue below.

Suzie: William's voice cracked when he had an audition for the school play.
Ben: How embarrassing! He must have <u>lost **face**</u> at that time.

L.M(표면적 의미)	F.M(비유적 의미)
체면을 잃다/체면을 지키다	to lose(<–> maintain) one's reputation; 체면을 잃다(구기다)<–> 체면을 지키다(창피를 면하다)

- History: 중국의 표현이 19세기 후반에 영어로 번역되면서 사용되기 시작함. 원래 중국의 표현에는 'lose face'의 반대 개념인 'save face'는 없었는데, 도입되는 과정에서 영어에서만 신조어로 만들어졌음.

♣ Make your own dialogue.

◎ fair and square

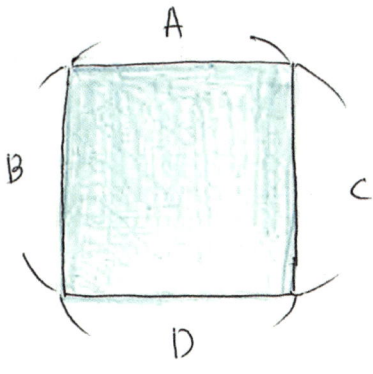

$A = B = C = D$

fair and square

- Guess the meaning of the idiom in the dialogue below.

Suzie: I'm upset we lost the game.

Ben: I know…. but let's try not to whine. At least, we lost it *fair and square*.

L.M(표면적 의미)	F.M(비유적 의미)
정사각형인	straightforwardly, in an honest manner; 직설적으로, 정직하게, 솔직히

- History: 17세기 이래로 fair와 square는 같은 의미로 쓰였는데, 같은 뜻을 지닌 동의어를 반복적으로 쓴 것임. 정사각형인 완벽하게 동등한 각도와 길이를 가진 Square는 어딘가가 꼬이거나 비틀어진 곳이 없이 '정직한'이란 의미를 시사하게 됨.

♣ Make your own dialogue.

⊙ a fat cat

- Guess the meaning of the idiom in the dialogue below.

Suzie: Did you see William's brand-new luxurious car?

Ben: Yeah! He's such a *fat* cat!

L.M(표면적 의미)	F.M(비유적 의미)
뚱뚱한 고양이	a very wealthy person, a highly rewarded executive; 아주 부유한 사람

- History: 미국에서는 비하하는 의미로 맵시 있고, 잘 먹고 살고, 자기만족에 도취한 고양이에 비유하여 fat cat이라고 말하였는데, 이는 특히 1920년대에 정당에 기부하는 자본주의자들을 일컬어 이렇게 불렀으며, 나아가 부자인 개개인을 지칭하는 것으로 넓게 사용되었음.

♣ Make your own dialogue.

⊙ to kill the fatted calf

- Guess the meaning of the idiom in the dialogue below.

Suzie: Sam's brother will be discharged from the army this weekend.
Ben: I heard that. His family must be killing the *fatted* calf for the welcoming party for him.

L.M(표면적 의미)	F.M(비유적 의미)
살찐 소를 죽이다	to celebrate (someone's return) with feasting; 잔치를 베풀며 (누군가의 귀환을) 축하하다

- History: 송아지는 축제(만찬)를 위해서 살찌우는데, 살찐 송아지를 죽인다는 것은 만찬을 준비하여 축하한다는 것을 의미함. 이는 예수님께서 말씀하신 Luke(누가복음) 중의 우화에서 인용된 말로서, 아버지의 재산을 탕진하고 돌아온 탕자를 보고 그의 귀환을 축하하기 위해서 기르던 소를 잡아 만찬을 준비했던 것에서 유래함.

♣ Make your own dialogue.

⊙ a **feather** in one's cap

a feather in one's cap

- Guess the meaning of the idiom in the dialogue below.

Suzie: The actress, Yoon won the Academy award for the best actress.
Ben: I'm very proud of her. This award is definitely a _feather_ in her cap.

L.M(표면적 의미)	F.M(비유적 의미)
모자 안에 깃털	credit; acknowledgement for one's work, achievement; 승인, 성취, 성과

- History: 여러 다른 문화권에서 보여지는 관습의 하나로써, 특히 미국의 인디언들 사이에서 가장 잘 알려져 있었던 것으로, 적군을 죽일 때마다 머리 위에 깃털을 꽂아서 표시했다는 데에서 유래함

♣ Make your own dialogue.

♣ as fit as a fiddle

- Guess the meaning of the idiom in the dialogue below.

Suzie: You look great today!

Ben: I'm as fit as a fiddle. I walk everyday nowadays.

L.M(표면적 의미)	F.M(비유적 의미)
바이올린의 현처럼 짱짱한	on top form, in excellent health; 컨디션이 최고인, 매우 건강한

- History: William Haughton의 연극인 *Englishmen for My Money*에 나왔던 직유법(비유 중 하나)이 쓰인 대사에서 유래함. 16세기에는 fiddle(바이올린의 현)은 악기뿐만 아니라 흥을 돋우는 사람인 fiddler에까지 사용되었는데, 바이올린의 짱짱한 현, 또는 분위기를 즐겁게 띄우는 상황에 딱 들어맞는 바이올린 연주자도 의미하였음. 'fit'이란 단어는 점차 신체적인 웰빙(복지, 안녕)의 의미와 동일하게 사용되었음.

♣ **Make your own dialogue.**

⊙ feet of clay

– Guess the meaning of the idiom in the dialogue below.

Suzie: Why the long face?

Ben: I made a few mistakes on the math test.

Suzie: You don't need to worry. You can learn from your mistakes. Even Lincoln had **_feet_ of clay**, you know.

L.M(표면적 의미)	F.M(비유적 의미)
진흙으로 된 발	a weakness perceived in someone held in high regard; 깊은 존경을 받는 사람에게 숨겨진 의외의 약점; 숨겨진 약점

– History: 성경 중 Daniel의 이야기에서 나온 말로, Daniel은 왕의 골칫거리였던 꿈을 해몽하게 되는데 꿈속에서 왕은 반짝거리며 빛나는 거대한 인간의 동상을 보았다고 함. 꿈에서 머리는 금으로 되어 있고 아래로 내려오는 부분은 철로 만들어졌으며, 그 동상의 발은 부분적으로 철과 진흙이 섞여 있었다고 함. 이에 대해서 Daniel이 신의 뜻으로 해석하기를 금을 나타내는 머리 부분은 강한 왕조의 시작을 뜻하나, 후세로 내려올수록 그 힘이 약해져서 왕조는 갈라지게 될 거라 예언하였음. 웅장해 보이는 동상은 보이는 것만큼 강하지 않았고 실은 약점을 가지고 있었다고 하는 데에서 유래함. 위대하고 가장 완벽해 보이는 것조차 숨겨진 결함이 있다는 것을 의미함.

♣ Make your own dialogue.

⊙ to have a finger in every pie

to have a finger
in every pie

- Guess the meaning of the idiom in the dialogue below.

Suzie: Sam got on my nerves again!

Ben: What happened?

Suzie: He said that I need to go on a diet asking if I gained some weight recently?

Ben: You know, he likes to <u>have a *finger* in every pie.</u>

L.M(표면적 의미)	F.M(비유적 의미)
모든 파이에 손가락을 대다	to play a part in many activities, to be meddlesome, interfering; 오지랖이 넓은/참견하는

- History: 파이가 맛있어 보일 때 살짝 맛보는 것을 참는 것은 매우 어려운 일임. 파이의 수가 많을수록, 그 유혹은 커짐. 여러 개의 파이에 손가락을 대어 보는 것은 다른 사람들의 일에 참견하고자 하는 인간의 본성을 반영한 표현임. 적인 웰빙(복지, 안녕)의 의미와 동일하게 사용되었음.

♣ Make your own dialogue.

Idioms from A to Z: F

⊙ to be all **fingers** and thumbs

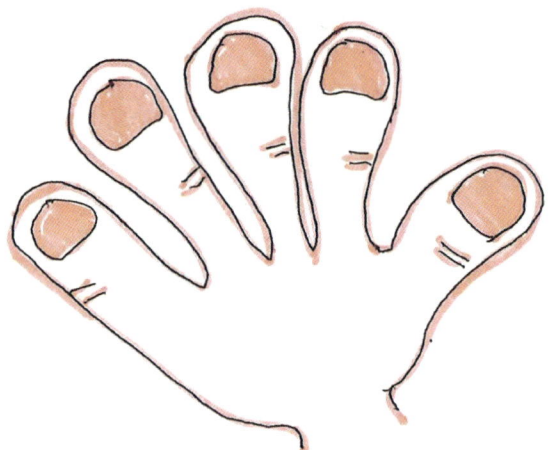

- Guess the meaning of the idiom in the dialogue below.

Suzie: William helped me to wash the dishes, but unfortunately, he dropped one of my mom's favorite plates and it broke. I was upset, but I couldn't say anything to him. Because you know, he didn't do it intentionally, so….

Ben: I see. William is a good boy except that he <u>is all *fingers* and thumbs.</u>

L.M(표면적 의미)	F.M(비유적 의미)
모든 손가락과 엄지손가락	to be very clumsy; 서툰/물건을 잘 떨어트리는

- History: 모든 손가락이 엄지손가락으로 되어 있다면 정교한 일을 완수하기에 서툴고 어색할 거라는 데에서 유래함.

♣ Make your own dialogue.

◉ a drink like a **fish** (to drink like a **fish**)

— Guess the meaning of the idiom in the dialogue below.

Ben: I need something to help soak up the alcohol.

Suzie: I warned you not to drink too much last night. You <u>drink like a *fish*.</u>

L.M(표면적 의미)	F.M(비유적 의미)
물고기처럼 마시기	to drink alcohol in excess; 지나치게 술을 마시는

— History: 물고기는 물속에서 입을 여닫을 때마다 물을 마시는 것 이외에는 하는 일이 없어 보일 정도로, 17세기 초부터 술을 많이 마시는 사람은 물고기에 비유되어 사용되었음.

♣ Make your own dialogue.

⊙ the flavour of the month

- Guess the meaning of the idiom in the dialogue below.

Ben: I love your neon T-shirt. It looks good on you. How stylish!

Suzie: Thanks. Neon color is <u>the *flavour* of the month</u> this summer season.

L.M(표면적 의미)	F.M(비유적 의미)
그 달의 맛	something temporarily in fashion, a fad; 일시적인 유행

- History:

1940년대에, 미국의 아이스크림 제조업체가 특별한 프로모션으로 이 달의 맛을 소개함으로써 소비자들이 더 많은 제품을 먹고 싶어 하도록 유혹하였던 데에서 유래함.

♣ **Make your own dialogue.**

⊙ to **fly** off the handle

– Guess the meaning of the idiom in the dialogue below.

Ben: Who ate my chocolate ice-cream, which I hid in the freezer. I was about to have it as a dessert after lunch.

Suzie: I saw William eating it a few minutes ago.

Ben: How could he?

Suzie: Calm down! Don't <u>*fly off the handle*</u> with this little thing.

Ben: You don't understand. I saved it for later for today.

L.M(표면적 의미)	F.M(비유적 의미)
손잡이가 날아가다	to lose one's temper; 흥분하다, 화내다

– History: 19세기 초 미국의 서부 개척자들 사이에서 쓰였던 표현으로, 손잡이가 헐거워진 도끼는 다음번에 세게 강타하면 날아가 버리게 되는데, 이런 방식으로 도끼가 망가지면 위험할 뿐만 아니라 다른 새로운 손잡이가 만들어질 때까지 일을 멈춰야 했다는 것을 의미함. 이러한 사건은 감정의 폭발과 예외 없이 연관되었고, 따라서 화난 행위는 도끼머리를 잃어버린 것과 연관 지을 수 있음.

♣ Make your own dialogue.

◉ to take French leave

- Guess the meaning of the idiom in the dialogue below.

Ben: Where were you at the party last night? I was looking for you, but I couldn't find you.

Suzie: I took **French** leave at 10 o'clock.

L.M(표면적 의미)	F.M(비유적 의미)
프랑스 방식으로 떠나다	to leave one's duties without permission, to leave without notice; 허락 없이 의무(행동)를 멈추다/그만두다/알리지 않고 떠나다

- History: 1차 세계 대전 때, 군대 사이에서는 'desert(버리다)'라는 의미로 통용되었는데, 그 유래는 18세기의 프랑스 사회에서 시작되었음. 프랑스에서는 파티를 연 주인에게 중간에 떠나는 것을 알리는 것은 예의가 아니라고 여기는 문화가 있었음. 영국 사회는 프랑스와는 반대로, 프랑스 사람들처럼 알리지 않고 모호하게 파티를 떠나는 행동을 달갑게 여기지 않았다고 전해짐.

♣ **Make your own dialogue.**

Idioms from A to Z: F

Idioms from A to Z: G

-G-

♣ These are the List of Idioms G. Are there any idioms you already know? If not, try to guess the meaning of the idioms below.

- to pick up the **gauntlet** ---------------------------- ☐
- to play to the **gallery** ---------------------------- ☐
- the **gift** of the **gab** ---------------------------- ☐
- the **gravy** train ---------------------------- ☐
- to **get** someone's **goat** ---------------------------- ☐
- to cook someone's **goose** ---------------------------- ☐
- (on/through) the **grapevine** ---------------------------- ☐
- It's all **Greek** to me ---------------------------- ☐
- the **green-eyed** monster ---------------------------- ☐
- to **grin** and bear it ---------------------------- ☐
- up a **gum** tree ---------------------------- ☐

⊙ to pick up the gauntlet

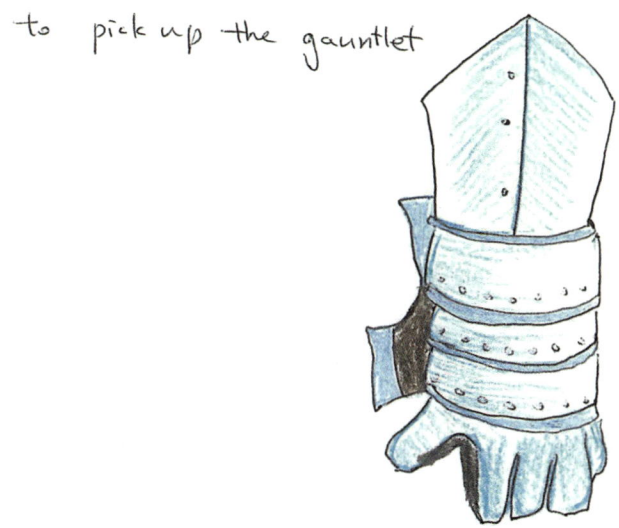

- Guess the meaning of the idiom in the dialogue below.

Ben: We lost the soccer game! It was a close game.

Suzie: I know. Let's practice more and pick up the gauntlet for the next match.

L.M(표면적 의미)	F.M(비유적 의미)
장갑을 집어 들다	pick up the gauntlet: 도전에 응하다(to accept a challenge) cf) throw down the gauntlet: 도전장을 내밀다 (던지다) (to issue a challenge)

- History: gauntlet은 갑옷 또는 튼튼한 장갑을 의미함. 갑옷이나 장갑을 챙기는 행동은 싸움(도전)에 응하는 것으로 받아들여짐. cf) throw down the gauntlet는 갑옷이나 장갑을 던지는 행동은 싸움에 도전한다는 의미로 받아들여짐

♣ Make your own dialogue.

⊙ to play to the gallery

− Guess the meaning of the idiom in the dialogue below.

Ben: Did you watch a new movie by the director, Bong Jun Ho?
Suzie: Yes, I really liked it.
Ben: I heard he <u>played to the *gallery*</u> when he wrote the scenario for this movie.

L.M(표면적 의미)	F.M(비유적 의미)
갤러리석을 향해서 연기하다	to perform/speak in a way intended to appeal to the less sophisticated members of an audience; 대중의 인기, 통속적 취향을 노리다(맞추다)

− History: 극장에서 가장 싼 자리를 gallery로 부르는데, gallery석을 향해서 연기를 한다는 뜻은 대중이나 통속적 취향(미)에 맞춘다는 뜻. The Guardian지의 기사 중에 "Trump <u>plays to the gallery</u> at CPAC and the gallery loves it."이란 제목이 쓰였는데, Trump 대통령이 통속적 대중을 이용하여 정치를 한다는 것을 꼬집는 기사를 다루었음. (2018.2.23.)

♣ Make your own dialogue.

Idioms from A to Z: G

⊙ the gift of the gab

- Guess the meaning of the idiom in the dialogue below.

Ben: I saw Will Smith slap Chris Rock in the face.

Suzie: It was shocking.

Ben: Even though he has the *gift* of the *gab*, this time his joke about Will's wife was too much.

Suzie: I know, but violence can't be forgiven under any circumstances.

L.M(표면적 의미)	F.M(비유적 의미)
입의 선물(재주)	the ability to talk fluently(about trivial matters); 말재주, 능변, (경멸적 의미로) 수다쟁이

- History: 'gab'은 스코틀랜드, 아일랜드에 기원을 둔 'mouth'의 의미를 가짐.

♣ Make your own dialogue.

⊙ the gravy train

- Guess the meaning of the idiom in the dialogue below.

Ben: I earned the money just from answering some survey questions.
Suzie: It's <u>the *gravy* train</u>!
Ben: Yeah, I realized I can sometimes make some money easily like this.

L.M(표면적 의미)	F.M(비유적 의미)
그레이비(소스) 기차	a job that commands a good profit for little effort; 적은 노력으로 이윤을 얻는 직업, 일하지 않고 얻은 보너스

- History: 식사 위에 '추가'적으로 부어진 소스를 'gravy'라고 부르는 데에서 유래함. 나중에 train이란 단어와 함께 쓰이기 시작하였는데, 일을 덜 하고도 같은 임금을 받을 수 있는, 노동이 비교적 쉬운 철로가 있는 철도 조차장을 의미하는 데에서 유래하기도 함.

♣ Make your own dialogue.

◎ to get someone's goat

- Guess the meaning of the idiom in the dialogue below.

Ben: Is there anything that **_gets_ your _goat?_**

Suzie: It gets my goat when I see someone drop litter in public.

L.M(표면적 의미)	F.M(비유적 의미)
누군가의 염소를 취하다	to irritate; annoy someone 짜증/초조하게 하다

- History: 원래 안정된 짝꿍으로서, 경마를 앞두고 초조한 경주마를 안정시키기 위해서 염소를 마사에 두었던 데에서 유래함. 또는 염소 자체가 짜증이 나면 들이받는 데에서도 유래한다고 함.

♣ **Make your own dialogue.**

Idioms from A to Z: G

◎ to cook someone's goose

- Guess the meaning of the idiom in the dialogue below.
Ben: Are the birthday party preparations for William going well?
Suzie: So far, so good. Don't mention anything to William!
Ben: I know. Don't worry. I won't **cook your goose**.

L.M(표면적 의미)	F.M(비유적 의미)
누군가의 거위를 요리하다	to ruin someone's plans or chances of success; 다른 사람의 계획 또는 성공 가능성을 망치다

- History: 1560년대 스웨덴의 Eric왕의 이야기에서 유래하였음. Eric왕은 소수의 군사만을 데리고 적지에 침투하였는데, 그때 적군은 그들을 경멸한다는 의미로 거위를 매달아 두었다고 함. 그 당시에는 거위를 매다는 행위는 상대방을 경멸한다는 뜻으로 여겨졌기 때문에 이를 보고 화가 난 Eric왕은 적군의 마을을 불태우게 했는데, 적진 마을 사람들이 왜 마을을 불태우려고 했냐고 물으니, 사실대로 말하지 않고 "거위를 요리하려고 그랬다"며 다른 핑계를 댔다고 함

♣ Make your own dialogue.

Idioms from A to Z: G

◉ (on/through) the grapevine

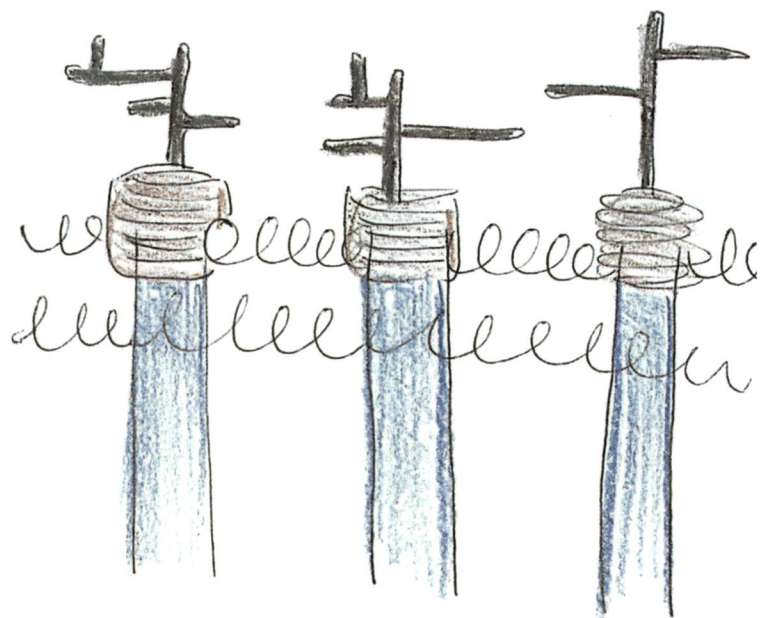

- Guess the meaning of the idiom in the dialogue below.
Ben: Are you leaving?
Suzie: Where did you hear that?
Ben: On the *grapevine.*

L.M(표면적 의미)	F.M(비유적 의미)
포도 덩굴을 통해서	gossip; rumour; 가십, 루머, 유언비어

- History: 1844년 Samuel Morse라는 사람이 워싱턴에서 볼티모어까지 'What God hath wrought'라는 첫 전보를 쳤다고 함. 처음 장거리 telegraph(전보)를 치기 위해서는 여기 저기에 전선을 연결할 전신주 등이 설치되었어야 했는데, 그 모습이 흡사 포도 덩굴처럼 뒤죽박죽되어 있었다는 데에서 유래하여 'grapevine telegraph'라고도 불렸음. 현재는 '출처를 알 수 없는 루머' 등을 의미하는 것으로 많이 쓰임.

♣ Make your own dialogue.

⊙ It's all Greek to me

It's all Greek to me.

– Guess the meaning of the idiom in the dialogue below.
Ben: Do you know what LTNS means? It is used on SNS.
Suzie: It's all *Greek* to me.
Ben: It stands for Long Time No See!
Suzie: I can't understand the language teenagers speak nowadays.

L.M(표면적 의미)	F.M(비유적 의미)
내게는 모두 그리스어 같다	I don't understand what is being said.; 뭐라는 말인지 못 알아듣겠다

– History: 셰익스피어의 연극인 *Julius Caesar*의 대사 중에서 유래하였음. 극 중 당시 로마에는 Caesar를 암살하려고 하는 Cassius와 Brutus 같은 사람들과 Caesar를 왕으로 추대해야 한다고 생각하는 두 부류가 있었는데, 그 시대의 최고의 석학이었던 Cicero(키케로)에게 끊임없이 그의 생각과 의견을 묻는 편지가 왔다고 함. Cassius는 Casca를 압박하여 Cicero가 한 말에 관해서 물어보는데, 그 대화에서 Cicero가 Greek(그리스어)로 말하였기 때문에 자신은 하나도 못 알아들었다고 말한 데에서 유래함.

♣ Make your own dialogue.

◉ the green-eyed monster

- Guess the meaning of the idiom in the dialogue below.

Ben: William bought the same jeans with mine.

Suzie: He tends to copy your fashion styles.

Ben: The <u>green-eyed</u> monster probably had him.

L.M(표면적 의미)	F.M(비유적 의미)
초록 눈의 괴물	jealousy, envy; 질투하는

- History: 14세기 넘어오면서 'being green'은 창백하고 감정적으로 괴로워하는 상태를 의미하였는데, 이것에 영감을 받은 셰익스피어가 *The Merchant of Venice*(베니스의 상인)에서 '질투를 하다'라는 뜻으로 'green-eyed'로, *Othello*에서 'the green-eyed monster'라는 표현을 사용한 데에서 유래함.

♣ Make your own dialogue.

♦ to grin and bear it

- Guess the meaning of the idiom in the dialogue below.

Ben: I'm stressed out because of the final exam coming up.

Suzie: Let's try to **grin and bear it** if we can't avoid the reality we face.

L.M(표면적 의미)	F.M(비유적 의미)
웃고 견뎌내다(참다)	to endure one's pain or difficulties without complaint; 불평 없이 고통이나 어려움을 견뎌내다

- History: 때때로 해결책이 없을 때는 한번 웃고 받아들여서 견뎌낸다는 의미로, 기분 좋음에 대한 부추김의 압박으로 받아들여질 수도 있지만, 실제로 원래 grin(소리 없이 활짝 웃다)이라는 뜻은 예전에는 smile(미소)라기보다는 grimace(찡그린 표정)을 뜻했었다고 함. 뮤지컬 *Matilda*에 나오는 노래인 'Naughty'의 가사 중에도 사용된 표현임.(Just because you find that life's not fair, it doesn't mean that you just have to *grin and bear it*.)

♣ Make your own dialogue.

◉ up a **gum** tree

- Guess the meaning of the idiom in the dialogue below.

Ben: I haven't finished the school project, yet. The due date is tomorrow, though.

Suzie: It takes quite a long time to finish it in my case. I guess you are <u>up a gum</u> tree to get it done in time.

L.M(표면적 의미)	F.M(비유적 의미)
고무(유칼립투스)나무 위에서	stuck in a difficult or embarrassing situation; 어려운 또는 황당한 상황에 빠진/처한

- History:

호주 영어에서 흔한 표현으로, 이 고무(gum)나무, 즉 이 유칼립투스(eucalyptus)나무는 호주의 3분의 2 이상을 차지한다고 함. 캘리포니아의 세쿼이아(sequoia) 나무의 높이를 넘을 정도로 키가 큰 것으로 유명함. 실제로 고공 다이빙을 했던 호주의 한 여성이 이 유칼립투스 나뭇가지에 떨어졌고, 나무의 높이가 너무 높은 나머지 그 여성을 구하기 위해 헬리콥터와 기술자들이 동원되었던 사건이 있다고 함.

♣ Make your own dialogue.

Idioms from A to Z: G

Idioms from A to Z: H

-H-

♣ These are the List of Idioms H. Are there any idioms you already know? If not, try to guess the meaning of the idioms below.

- living (from) **hand** to mouth ☐
- the **hair** of the dog ☐
- to let one's **hair** down ☐
- win (something) **hands** down ☐
- **hang(hold)** fire ☐
- **happy hunting** grounds ☐
- **house** of cards ☐
- go **haywire** ☐
- **hide**/bury one's **head** in the sand ☐
- a clean bill of **health** ☐

- in seventh **heaven** ---------------------------------- ☐
- **hold** your **horses** ---------------------------------- ☐
- at the eleventh **hour** ---------------------------------- ☐

◉ living (from) **hand** to mouth

- Guess the meaning of the idiom in the dialogue below.

Ben: I'm living *hand* to mouth nowadays. It has been almost a year since I quit my job.

Suzie: You need to find a new job a.s.a.p.

L.M(표면적 의미)	F.M(비유적 의미)
손에서 입으로 (끼니를 때우며) 살다	하루살이 생활을 하다, 겨우 견디며 살다

- History: 16세기에 봉건제도의 몰락, 인구 증가, 가축 사육으로 인한 농장 감소, 긴 내전 등으로 사회의 큰 문제로 '가난'이 대두된 데에서 유래함. 사람들은 내일을 생각할 겨를도 없이 당장 오늘 굶어 죽지 않기 위해서 버둥거렸음. 오늘날에는 즉각적인 배고픔보다는, 내일에 대한 계획이나 낮은 수입 등으로 오늘만을 생각하고 사는 상황을 가리킴.

♣ Make your own dialogue.

◉ the hair of the dog

- Guess the meaning of the idiom in the dialogue below.

Ben: I drank too much alcohol last night.
Suzie: Here is <u>the *hair* of the dog</u> for you.

L.M(표면적 의미)	F.M(비유적 의미)
개털	a tot of alcohol as a remedy for a hangover; 숙취 해소를 위한 치료 약으로써의 알코올 한 모금(적은 양)

- History: 고대의 치료 방법으로 개에게서 물리면 그 문 개의 털을 상처 부위에 두면 그 상처가 치유된다고 믿음. 16세기에 들어와서 이러한 방법이 숙취에도 적용이 되어서 술에 취한 다음 날 같은 종류의 술을 조금 마시면 숙취가 없어진다고 여겨짐. 미드나 영화에 나오는 대사 중에 등장인물이 숙취 해소를 위해 다음 날 술을 마시는 장면에 자주 사용되고 있는 표현임.

♣ Make your own dialogue.

◉ to let one's hair down

- Guess the meaning of the idiom in the dialogue below.

Ben: It was nice to chat with you over the phone last night.

Suzie: I am happy I got to know you better, too. We can let our *hair* down from now on.

L.M(표면적 의미)	F.M(비유적 의미)
머리를 풀어 내리다	to lose one's inhibitions; 스스럼없이 지내다, 릴렉스하며 즐기다

- History: 19세기 중반에 파티에 참가한 여성은 긴 올린 머리에 장식을 하고 나타나곤 했는데, 자신의 침실 방에 돌아가서야 머리를 아래로 풀 수 있는 것이 허락되었다는 데에서 유래하여, 친밀하게 스스럼없이 된 상태를 의미함.

♣ Make your own dialogue.

Idioms from A to Z: H

⊙ win (something) **hands down**

- Guess the meaning of the idiom in the dialogue below.

Ben: Team Korea won the Curling game on the final match.
Suzie: Our team won *hands* down.

L.M(표면적 의미)	F.M(비유적 의미)
손을 내린 상태로 이기다	to win with great ease; 아주 쉽게 이기다

- History: 경마 중, 경주의 끝에 다다르면 자신의 승리를 확신하는 기수는 말의 고삐를 늦추고 손을 떨어뜨린다는 데에서 유래함.

♣ Make your own dialogue.

⊙ hang(hold) fire

- Guess the meaning of the idiom in the dialogue below.

Ben: Didn't you say you were on a diet?
Suzie: I will start it from tomorrow.
Ben: Don't *hang fire.*

L.M(표면적 의미)	F.M(비유적 의미)
늦게 발사되다	to hesitate, to delay; 주저하다, 미루다

- History: 총기를 사용하던 시대에는 군인들이나 스포츠맨들은 총에 화약을 채우는 역할을 담당하였는데, 화약의 질이 떨어지거나 젖어 있으면 총을 점화하지 못하고 기다렸어야(hang) 한다는 데에서 유래함.

♣ Make your own dialogue.

Idioms from A to Z: H

◉ happy hunting grounds

- Guess the meaning of the idiom in the dialogue below.

Ben: It's so good to eat every meal for free here.

Suzie: There are **happy hunting grounds**. This is the reason why I like a cruise trip.

L.M(표면적 의미)	F.M(비유적 의미)
행복한 사냥터	death, heaven; 북미 인디언 무사의 천국, 만물이 풍성한 곳

- History: 미국 인디언들은 사후에 용감한 사냥꾼과 훌륭한 전사들은 사냥과 잔치로 가득 차 있고 즐길 수 있는 장소에 살 수 있다고 믿었다는 데에서 유래함.

♣ Make your own dialogue.

◉ house of cards

- Guess the meaning of the idiom in the dialogue below.

Ben: I'm making a plan about how to get into a university I wish to attend.
Suzie: It's a *house of cards* if you don't have good plans.

L.M(표면적 의미)	F.M(비유적 의미)
카드로 만든 집	an unsound plan, an insubstantial organization; 엉성하고 불안정한 계획

- History: 아이들이 카드로 집을 짓는 게임에서 유래하였는데, 입김 한번에도 쉽게 무너질 수 있는 카드로 지은 집이란 데에서 엉성하고 불안한 상태를 나타냄. House of Cards는 정치 주제를 다룬 인기가 높았던 미드의 제목이기도 함.

♣ Make your own dialogue.

⊙ go haywire

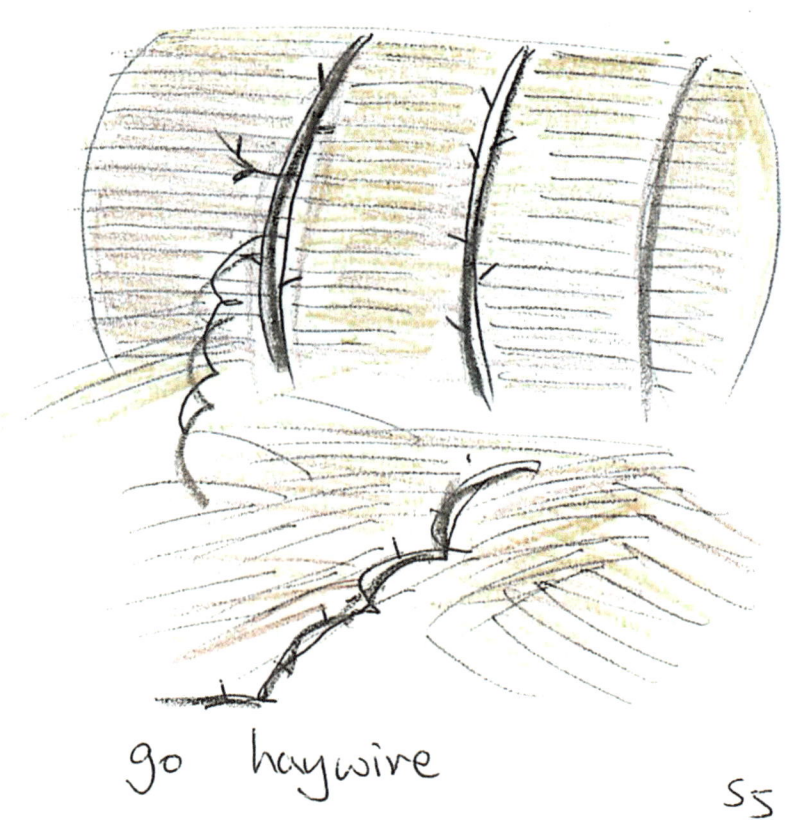

- Guess the meaning of the idiom in the dialogue below.

Ben: How is the party preparation going on?

Suzie: It is going haywire, I guess.

Ben: Why?

Suzie: There are too many different opinions about it.

L.M(표면적 의미)	F.M(비유적 의미)
뒤엉킨 상태가 되다	to go wrong, to be out of order, to go completely out of control; (일이) 잘못되다, 무질서한 상태인

- History: 20세기 초반 미국에서는 건초를 묶는 철사로 기계부터 울타리까지 고치는 데 많이 쓰였는데, 게으른 농장의 주인들은 관리를 소홀히 하여 철사가 빨리 녹슬었고 그 결과 지저분하고 무질서한 상태가 된 데에서 유래함.

♣ Make your own dialogue.

⊙ hide/bury one's head in the sand

— Guess the meaning of the idiom in the dialogue below.

Ben: We need to find a way to slow down Global Warming.

Suzie: I know. It's too sad that there are still some countries that <u>bury their heads in the sand</u> in this matter.

Ben: We have to cooperate with each other to solve this problem.

Suzie: You can say that again!

L.M(표면적 의미)	F.M(비유적 의미)
머리를 모래 속에 숨기다/묻다	to ignore a difficulty, to pretend a problem does not exist; 문제가 존재하지 않은 체하기 위해서 어려움을 무시하다 e.g.) head-in-the-sand policy

— History: 이것은 타조의 이솝 우화에서 빗대어진 것인데, 위험을 감지하면 자신의 머리를 모래 속에 숨기는 데에서 유래함.

♣ Make your own dialogue.

a clean bill of health

- Guess the meaning of the idiom in the dialogue below.

Ben: Where are you heading now?

Suzie: I'm going to the hospital for a regular check-up. Hope the doctor will give me a clean bill of *health.* Wish me luck!

Ben: Sure. Good luck!

L.M(표면적 의미)	F.M(비유적 의미)
건강 증명서	an assurance, after close scrutiny, that there are no irregularities - financial, moral, etc.; 건강함을 증명하는 보험서, 불법 사항이 없다는 확언/보험

- History: 17세기에 특히 유럽에서는 배가 항구에 정박하기 위해서는 배가 출발했을 때, 전염병으로부터 안전하다는 증명하는 증서를 요구한 데에서 유래함. 현재는 엄격한 조사 후에 불법 사항이 발견되지 않았다는 것을 증명한다는 의미로 많이 쓰임.

♣ Make your own dialogue.

Idioms from A to Z: H

◉ in seventh **heaven**

- Guess the meaning of the idiom in the dialogue below.

Ben: Now that Sam has been promoted.

Suzie: He must be in seventh *heaven*, now.

L.M(표면적 의미)	F.M(비유적 의미)
일곱 번째 천국에서	in ecstasy, in sheer delight; 황홀함 속에, 큰 기쁨을 느끼는

- History: 고대의 유대인과 무슬림들의 사고로는 7개의 행성의 궤도에 해당하는 7개의 혼천의(구) 속으로 하늘이 나뉘었음(7은 완벽한 숫자로 여겨졌음), 죽은 자는 이생에서 어떻게 살았는지에 따라서 심판을 받고 적절한 보상의 수준의 하늘의 장소로 보내어졌는데, 가장 높은 레벨이 바로 천사와 신이 살고 있는 7번째의 천국이었다는 데에서 유래함.(*In Seventh Heaven*라는 미국 TV 시리즈가 인기를 끌기도 했음.)

♣ Make your own dialogue.

Idioms from A to Z: H

⊙ hold your horses

- Guess the meaning of the idiom in the dialogue below.

Ben: Why are you in such a hurry! *Hold your horses*! We've got plenty of time.
Suzie: Let's do it step by step.

L.M(표면적 의미)	F.M(비유적 의미)
너의 말을 잡아라!	restrain yourself, be patient; 너 자신을 자제하라, 참을성을 가져라

- History: 막 출발하려는 데에 성격이 급하고 안달이 난 말들을 저지하기 위한 명령으로 쓰였던 데에서 유래함. 비유적으로 잔뜩 긴장하거나 화가 나 있거나 좌절한 사람을 달래 주기 위해서 쓰임.

♣ Make your own dialogue.

⊙ at the eleventh hour

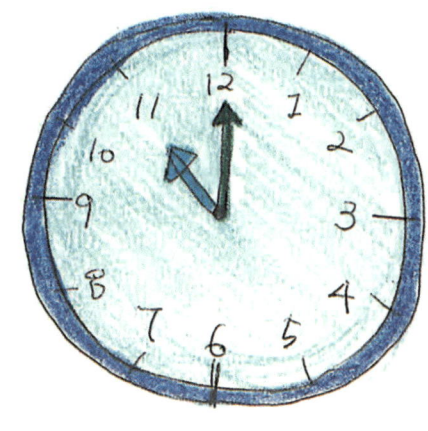

- Guess the meaning of the idiom in the dialogue below.

Ben: Did you submit your application form for the audition?

Suzie: Yes, at the eleventh *hour!*

L.M(표면적 의미)	F.M(비유적 의미)
11번째의 시간	at the very last moment; 마지막 기회에, 막다른 판에

- History: 마태복음 중 노동자들의 우화 기록에서 유래한 것으로, 집주인은 자신의 포도밭에서 일할 노동자들을 고용하였는데, 그들을 각각 다른 시간대에 일하게 하였는데, 마지막 11번째 시간에 일하던 사람들 모두에게도 같은 임금을 지급하였음. 이 일화에서, 예수님께서 말씀하시기를 '신은 그에게 다가오는 모든 이들, 심지어 죽음 직전에 다가오고 신을 따르는 사람에게조차도 똑같이 받아들여 주신다'고 함.

♣ Make your own dialogue.

Idioms from A to Z: I

-I-

♣ These are the List of Idioms I. Are there any idioms you already know? If not, try to guess the meaning of the idioms below.

- ⊙ to break the **ice** -- ☐
- ⊙ the tip of the **iceberg** ------------------------------ ☐
- ⊙ the spitting **image** of / very spit / the dead spit ---------- ☐
- ⊙ to add **insult** to **injury** -------------------------------- ☐
- ⊙ an **iron** hand in a velvet glove ------------------------ ☐
- ⊙ to have (too) many **irons** in the fire -------------------- ☐
- ⊙ an **ivory** tower -- ☐

⊙ to break the ice

break the ice

- Guess the meaning of the idiom in the dialogue below.

Ben: How was your new class? Do you like your classmates?
Suzie: My homeroom teacher got us to do some games so that we could <u>break the ice</u> and get to know each other better.

L.M(표면적 의미)	F.M(비유적 의미)
얼음을 깨다	to break down social awkwardness and formality; 사회적 어색함과 의례적 형식을 깨트리다

- History: 강이나 해협의 딱딱한 얼음을 깨트리기 위해서 특별히 만들어진 선박에서 유래하여, 비유적으로 딱딱한 얼음의 이미지에서 딱딱한 분위기를 깬다는 뜻으로 쓰이게 됨.

♣ Make your own dialogue.

Idioms from A to Z: I

⊙ the tip of the iceberg

− Guess the meaning of the idiom in the dialogue below.

Ben: I think I left my bag in the subway.
Suzie: Sorry to hear that. Did you visit the Lost and Found?
Ben: I will, but you know what? Losing the bag is just <u>the tip of the *iceberg*</u>.
　　　All of the important stuff was in there.
Suzie: I hope you can find it back.

L.M(표면적 의미)	F.M(비유적 의미)
빙산의 일각	an unpleasant problem which is just the first phase of a much larger and even more difficult situation; 새로운 국면의 실제로 더 크고 어려운 상황의 불쾌한 문제

− History: 빙산 대부분은 바다 밑에 있고 극히 일부분만이 바다 위에 나와 보인다는 데에서 유래함. the tip(끝)이 들어간 다른 표현으로는 "<u>on the tip of the tongue</u>(생각이 날 듯 말 듯 해!)"가 있는데, 이는 혀끝에서 맴돌며 말로 잘 표현되지 않는, 즉 '설단 현상'을 나타냄. 시험과 같은 심리적 압박을 심하게 느끼는 경우, 어떤 정보가 장기 기억에는 존재하지만, 정보에 정확히 접근이 불가하여 기억을 인출하는 데 어려움을 겪는 상황에서 주로 나타남.

♣ **Make your own dialogue.**

Idioms from A to Z: I

◎ the spitting image of / very spit / the dead spit

- Guess the meaning of the idiom in the dialogue below.

Ben: I saw your father on the street yesterday.
Suzie: How come you are so sure about it? I don't think I have introduced him to you before.
Ben: You are <u>the spitting *image* of</u> him.

L.M(표면적 의미)	F.M(비유적 의미)
침을 뱉어 놓은 듯한 모습	the exact likeness of; 완전히 빼닮음, 판박이 = a chip off the old block

- History: spit은 '뱉다(침을)/뱉음'이란 의미가 있어 한 사람이 다른 사람을 뱉어 놓은 듯이 고스란히 닮았다는 데에서 유래하여 'spit'은 'likeness(닮음)'이란 의미도 갖게 됨. 특히 이 표현은 미국의 남부 지방에서 많이 사용되었는데 남부 사람들의 발음 특성상 'r'을 약하게 발음하는 것을 감안하면 'spit'은 'spirit'에서 온 것으로 볼 수도 있음. 예컨대 'My daughter is <u>*the very spirit and image of*</u> his father.' 이 문장은 내 딸은 마음(영혼)과 외모 둘 다, 즉 겉과 속이 모두 아빠를 빼닮았다는 의미로 해석할 수 있음.

♣ **Make your own dialogue.**

⊙ to add **insult** to **injury**

- Guess the meaning of the idiom in the dialogue below.

Ben: You look upset. What's wrong?

Suzie: I had a bad day at school today. <u>To add *insult* to *injury*</u>, I was scolded by my mom at home.

L.M(표면적 의미)	F.M(비유적 의미)
상처에 모욕을 더하다	to upset someone further with a second insensitive act or remark; 무감각한 행동이나 말을 더하여 사람의 기분을 더 언짢게 만들다; 설상가상으로(from bad to worse)

- History: 이솝 우화 중 *Baldman and the Fly*(대머리와 파리)라는 이야기에서 대머리 부분을 문 파리를 잡기 위해서 찰싹 때려서 잡으려고 시도하였는데, 보통의 경우가 그렇듯 파리는 도망가고 더더욱 그 파리를 잡고 싶게 되었다는 데에서 유래함.

♣ Make your own dialogue.

Idioms from A to Z: I

◉ an iron hand in a velvet glove

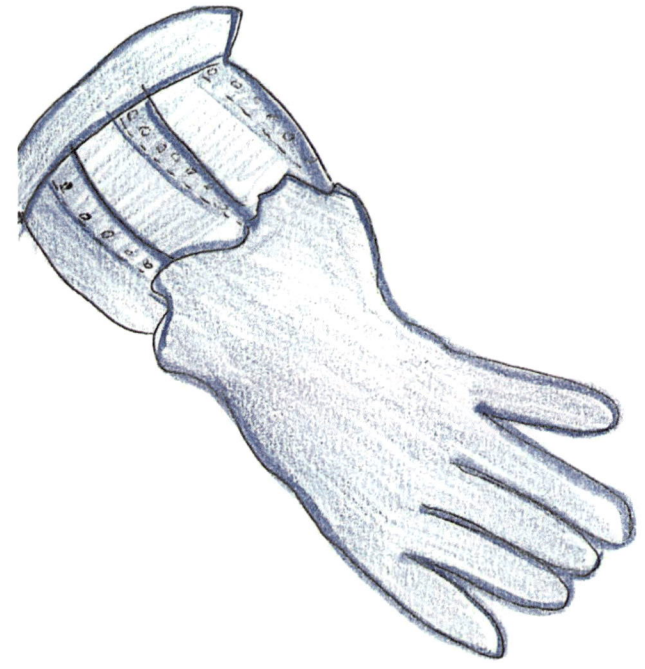

an iron hand in a velvet glove

- Guess the meaning of the idiom in the dialogue below.

Ben: The new principal looks very gentle.

Suzie: The rumor says that he also has an *iron* hand in a velvet glove.

L.M(표면적 의미)	F.M(비유적 의미)
벨벳 장갑 안에 철(무쇠) 손	firm and inflexible in leadership, beneath a veneer of gentleness; 부드러운 겉치장 아래에 확고하고 완강한 리더십(외유내강)

- History: 부드러운 벨벳 장갑 속에 철로 된 손의 이미지를 연상하듯이 바깥은 부드러우나, 속 안은 딱딱하고 강한 것을 묘사함. Thomas Carlyle가 *Latter Day Pamphlets*에서 Napoleon의 성정을 묘사하는 장면에서 유래함. 보통 통치하는 정치 지도자를 묘사하는 데 쓰였으며, 스페인 국왕이었던 Charles 5세에 대한 묘사에도 쓰임. 최근에는 일반적인 사람의 성격을 묘사하는 데에도 많이 쓰이고 있음.

♣ Make your own dialogue.

⊙ to have (too) many irons in the fire

- Guess the meaning of the idiom in the dialogue below.
Ben: I think you have too many irons in the fire recently.
Suzie: Yes, actually I'm stressed out because of that.

L.M(표면적 의미)	F.M(비유적 의미)
불 속에 너무 많은 다리미를 가지고 있다	to have (too) many projects in hand, undertaking to be attended to; 손대는 일이 너무 많은

- History: 대장장이들은 불 속에서 철을 주조하기 위해서 주의 깊게 철을 다뤄야 하는데, 불 속에 너무 많은 철을 넣고 주조하려 하면 충분한 주의를 기울이지 못하게 된다는 데에서 유래함. 또는 예전에는 세탁소에서 쇠다리미를 쓸 때 석탄불 속에 넣어서 데워서 사용하였는데 너무 많은 쇠다리미를 넣으면 다리미의 철이 너무 달아올라 옷을 태우게 되었다는 데에서 유래함.

♣ Make your own dialogue.

Idioms from A to Z: I

◎ an ivory tower

- Guess the meaning of the idiom in the dialogue below.

Ben: I've finished my project and submitted it.

Suzie: You should get some rest.

Ben: I will. Do you have <u>an *ivory* tower</u> for my vacation?

L.M(표면적 의미)	F.M(비유적 의미)
상아로 된 탑	a sheltered existence away from the problems and practicalities of life, an attitude of aloofness from the realities of life; 문젯거리나 현실성에서 멀리 떨어져 있는 쉴 곳; 안식처/삶의 현실에서 초탈한 삶의 태도

- History: 프랑스의 로맨틱한 시인이자 작가인 Alfred de Vigny가 실제의 삶에서 실망과 좌절을 경험하고 난 뒤, 나중에는 결국 사회에서 고립된 장소에서 혼자 보내며 글을 쓰게 되었다는 데에서 유래함. 나중에는 Henri Bergson이 영어로 번역하여 영어에서도 사용됨.

♣ Make your own dialogue.

Idioms from A to Z: I

Idioms from A to Z: J

-J-

♣ These are the List of Idioms J. Are there any idioms you already know? If not, try to guess the meaning of the idioms below.

◉ a **jack** of all trades ---------------------------------- ☐

◉ to hit the **jackpot** ---------------------------------- ☐

◉ **Janus**-faced ---------------------------------- ☐

◉ **jam** tomorrow ---------------------------------- ☐

◉ with **jaundiced** eye ---------------------------------- ☐

◉ the cut of someone's **jib** ---------------------------------- ☐

◉ to **jockey** for position ---------------------------------- ☐

◉ a **job**'s comforter ---------------------------------- ☐

◉ to keep up with the **Joneses** ---------------------------------- ☐

◉ to **jump** the gun ---------------------------------- ☐

⊙ a jack of all trades

- Guess the meaning of the idiom in the dialogue below.

Ben: William helped me fix my bike.
Suzie: He also helped me fix my laptop.
Ben: Yes, he is a *jack* of all trades.

L.M(표면적 의미)	F.M(비유적 의미)
무엇이든지 하는 잭(Jack)	a person who can turn his hand to anything; 만물박사

- History: Jack이라는 이름은 오랫동안 영어권에서 평범한 사람을 뜻하는 일반적인 이름으로 불리어 왔음. 처음 여러 작품에서는 거래 등을 성사시키지 못하는 능력이 부족한 사람을 뜻하는 부정적인 의미로 사용되었으나, 현재에는 단순히 무엇이든지 하는 사람을 뜻하게 됨.

♣ Make your own dialogue.

⊙ to hit the jackpot

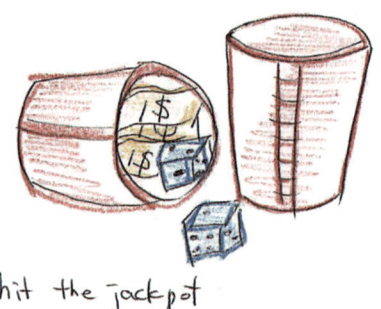

hit the jackpot

- Guess the meaning of the idiom in the dialogue below.

Ben: How was your trip to Vegas?
Suzie: My friend hit the jackpot. She earned $10,000.
Ben: Wow, good for her!

L.M(표면적 의미)	F.M(비유적 의미)
jackpot(항아리 그릇)을 터트리다	to win a large prize; 대박을 터트리다

- History: jackpot은 카드놀이에서 만들어진 단어로, 좋은 패를 내놓을 때까지 돈을 쌓아 두는 항아리 그릇을 뜻함. jackpot을 친다는 것은 그 안의 돈을 딴다는 뜻으로, 현재에는 카드놀이뿐 아니라 복권, 상 등 큰 재정적인 성공을 거둘 때 사용됨.

♣ Make your own dialogue.

⊙ Janus-faced

Janus-faced

- Guess the meaning of the idiom in the dialogue below.

Ben: I saw Tom bully a boy in my classroom today.
Suzie: Really? I thought he is the nicest guy that I've ever met.
Ben: Maybe he is *Janus-faced*.

L.M(표면적 의미)	F.M(비유적 의미)
야누스 얼굴을 한	hypocritical; 두 얼굴을 지닌, 위선적인

- History: Janus는 로마의 신이자 우주를 지키는 문지기 역할을 하였음. 시작과 끝을 나타내는 신으로, 머리의 앞과 뒤에 다른 얼굴을 지니고 있어서 앞과 뒤를 동시에 볼 수 있었다고 함.

♣ Make your own dialogue.

⊙ jam tomorrow

- Guess the meaning of the idiom in the dialogue below.

Ben: If you help me, I will get you a luxurious item.

Suzie: You always say that, but you haven't kept your words. What you're saying sounds like *jam tomorrow* to me.

Ben: Trust me this time.

L.M(표면적 의미)	F.M(비유적 의미)
잼은 내일	a promise of good things to come which rarely appear; (약속뿐인, 실현되지 않는) 행복한 미래

- History: Lewis Carroll이 쓴 이상한 나라의 앨리스 시리즈에서 언급된 말로써, 앨리스는 White 여왕이 옷을 입는 것을 돕고, 그 대가로 일주일에 2펜스와 하루걸러 한 번씩 잼을 받기로 하였는데, '하루걸러'라는 의미가 어제 또는 내일을 의미하고 절대 오늘이 될 수 없다는 데에서 '이룰 수 없는 미래'를 뜻하는 말로 쓰이게 됨.

Queen: You couldn't have it if you did want it. The rule is *jam tomorrow* and jam yesterday but never jam today.

Alice: I don't care for jam and don't want any today.

♣ **Make your own dialogue.**

◉ with jaundiced eye

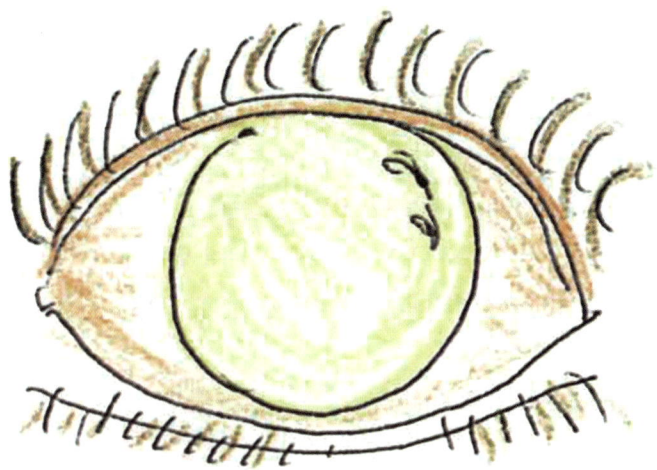

– Guess the meaning of the idiom in the dialogue below.

Ben: Isn't Jen a punk in school?

Suzie: What makes you say so?

Ben: Her looks such as dyed hair, piercing…. etc.

Suzie: Maybe she looks like a punk, but don't look on her **with *jaundiced eye*** before we get to know her better.

L.M(표면적 의미)	F.M(비유적 의미)
노란(황갈색의) 눈으로	taking a cynical, resentful view; 삐딱한 시선으로

– History: Jaundice는 간이 나빠 생기는 황달 증세를 뜻하는 말로, 보통 눈의 흰자가 노랗게 변하는 증상임. Jaundice는 프랑스어로 'yellow'를 뜻하고, 노랑은 '질투하는', '분개하는' 성격을 뜻하기도 함. 따라서 노란빛의 눈으로 세상을 바라본다는 것은 비유적으로 세상을 삐딱하게 바라본다는 의미로 쓰이게 됨.

♣ Make your own dialogue.

⊙ the cut of someone's jib

- Guess the meaning of the idiom in the dialogue below.

Ben: I like the cut of your *jib* today.

Suzie: Thanks for your compliment.

L.M(표면적 의미)	F.M(비유적 의미)
누군가의 삼각돛 스타일	someone's personal appearance or manner; 풍채, 외모, 첫인상

- History: 원래는 항해사들 사이에서 쓰이던 은어적인 표현이었으나, 현재는 더욱 일반적으로 많이 쓰이고 있음. jib은 뱃머리로부터 나와 있는 삼각형의 돛으로, 배가 항해하거나 선박하러 들어올 때 가장 먼저 보이는 부분으로, 이 jib을 보고, 어느 배인지를 인식할 수 있었다고 함.

♣ Make your own dialogue.

⊙ to **jockey** for position

- Guess the meaning of the idiom in the dialogue below.

Ben: Why are you in such a hurry?

Suzie: I have to go to a restaurant that newly opened. It doesn't get any reservation. To **jockey** for position, I have to get there as early as possible.

L.M(표면적 의미)	F.M(비유적 의미)
좋은 위치를 위해 다투다	유리한 자리를 차지하려고 다투다

- History: 17세기부터 Jockey는 말의 기수이면서도 동시에 말 장수였는데, 말 장수는 교활한 사기 행위로 잘 알려진 부도덕한 사람들로 알려짐. 'jockey'란 단어는 다른 사람에게서 유리한 자리를 차지하거나 다른 사람의 선수를 친다는 의미로 쓰이게 됨.

♣ Make your own dialogue.

⊙ a job's comforter

– Guess the meaning of the idiom in the dialogue below.

Ben: You look upset, today. What's wrong?

Suzie: I had a terrible day at school today. Jessi told me to forget about it saying I was too sensitive. That made me angrier. She was <u>a Job's comforter</u> to me.

L.M(표면적 의미)	F.M(비유적 의미)
욥(Job)을 위로하는 사람들	상대방을 위로하지만 오히려 그 위로로 상대의 기분을 더욱 망치는 사람

– History: 구약성경의 족장 Job의 이야기에서 유래함. 하나님은 하나님을 섬기는 Job을 시험하시기 위해서 사탄에게 Job에게 괴로움을 주도록 하는데, Job은 무리들, 하인들, 가족 모두 잃고 괴로워하지만 절대 하나님을 원망하지 않았다고 함. Job은 세 명의 친구로부터 그의 상황에 대해서 상담하였는데, 그들은 결국 Job의 걱정만 더욱 키웠다고 함. 여기에서 Job을 위로하는 사람들(comforters)은 그를 위로해 준다는 가면을 쓰고 결국에는 그에게 괴로움을 더욱 가중시키는 사람들을 뜻하게 되었다고 함.

♣ **Make your own dialogue.**

⊙ to keep up with the **Joneses**

- Guess the meaning of the idiom in the dialogue below.

Ben: Did you buy a new cellphone again?

Suzie: Yepp. I liked William's new phone.

Ben: Your old phone was quite a brand-new one, wasn't it? Don't <u>keep up with the *Joneses!*</u>

L.M(표면적 의미)	F.M(비유적 의미)
Joneses를 따라잡으려고 하다	to endeavour to keep up financially and socially with one's friends and neighbors; 남에게 뒤처지지 않으려고 노력하다

- History: New York Globe에 실린 Arther R Momand라는 만화가가 그린 *Keeping up with the Joneses*라는 만화가 있었는데, McGinis 가족의 일상생활과 고군분투를 다룬 내용이었음. 그들의 이웃인 Joneses는 만화에 실제로 등장하지는 않았지만, 만화 속에서 언제나 부러운 삶을 사는 사람으로 쭉 언급되었던 인물이었음.

♣ Make your own dialogue.

◉ to jump the gun

- Guess the meaning of the idiom in the dialogue below.

Ben: I think I did a good job in the job interview. I may get a job this time finally.

Suzie: I hope so…. but don't *jump the gun* for now!

L.M(표면적 의미)	F.M(비유적 의미)
총소리에 뛰쳐나가다	to embark upon a course of action too hastily, at an inappropriate time, to take an unfair advantage; 섣불리 행동하다, 김칫국부터 마시다; 불공정한 이득을 취하다

- History: 달리기 시합은 권총 사격 소리로부터 시작되는데, 권총 소리가 들리기 전에 미리 뛰쳐나가는 선수를 지칭하는 데에서 유래함.

♣ Make your own dialogue.

Idioms from A to Z: K

-K-

♣ These are the List of Idioms K. Are there any idioms you already know? If not, try to guess the meaning of the idioms below.

- ⊙ a **kettle** of fish -- ☐
- ⊙ to **kick** against the pricks ------------------------------ ☐
- ⊙ to **kick** over the traces -------------------------------- ☐
- ⊙ to **kick** the bucket ------------------------------------- ☐
- ⊙ to **kill** (someone) with **kindness** --------------------- ☐
- ⊙ (till) **Kingdom** come ----------------------------------- ☐
- ⊙ the **kiss** of death ------------------------------------- ☐
- ⊙ everything but the **kitchen** sink ----------------------- ☐
- ⊙ **knee-high** to a grasshopper --------------------------- ☐
- ⊙ to **knuckle** under -------------------------------------- ☐

◎ a kettle of fish

- Guess the meaning of the idiom in the dialogue below.
Ben: Did you figure out how you solve this problem?
Suzie: It's a _kettle_ of fish. I have no idea. Please help me

L.M(표면적 의미)	F.M(비유적 의미)
물고기가 들어 있는 양동이	a mess, a problem, a predicament; 엉망진창인 상태, 문제, 곤경

- History: 스코틀랜드의 강변에서 했던 피크닉의 한 유형에서 유래한 것으로, 피크닉에 온 손님들은 kettle이라고 부르는 커다란 철로 된 양동이에 강변에서 잡은 연어를 집어던져서 함께 조리하며 먹었다고 함. 마구 집어넣어진 kettle 속의 잡힌 물고기의 모습에서 연상됨.

♣ Make your own dialogue.

⊙ to kick against the pricks

− Guess the meaning of the idiom in the dialogue below.

Ben: For having lost the last soccer match. Many of us think the judge was somewhat unfair to us.

Suzie: Don't even think of attacking him, it will <u>kick against the pricks.</u> Just face the music.

L.M(표면적 의미)	F.M(비유적 의미)
뾰족한 것에 대항하여 걷어차다	to persist in useless resistance, to one's own cost; 긁어 부스럼을 만들다, 덤벼서 손해 보다

− History: 성경의 사도행전에 보면 사울이 기독교도를 벌주기 위해서 다마스쿠스로 떠나는 길에 하늘로부터 빛을 보게 되고 나중에 기독교도가 된다는 구절이 나오는데, 그 빛은 예수님을 의미하고, "나는 네가 핍박하는 예수라, 가시덤불을 걷어찰 수는 없느니라.(I am Jesus whom you are persecuting; it is hard for you to <u>kick against the pricks.</u>)"라는 구절이 있음. 마부가 신발 뒷굽의 박차로 말을 때릴 때 말이 저항하거나, 황소가 목동의 막대기에 저항하는 모습을 나타냄.

♣ **Make your own dialogue.**

Idioms from A to Z: K

⊙ to kick over the traces

- Guess the meaning of the idiom in the dialogue below.

Ben: Don't you think William **kicks** over the traces nowadays?

Suzie: I felt that way, too. He seems to be going through his puberty.

L.M(표면적 의미)	F.M(비유적 의미)
봇줄(trace) 위로 해서 걷어차다	to become reckless, out of control, to rebel; 제멋대로 굴다

- History: traces는 말을 뒤에 끄는 마차랑 연결하는 부분으로, 일하기 싫어하는 말은 trace 위에 다리를 두어 마부가 조종하기 힘들게 했다는 데에서 유래함.

♣ Make your own dialogue.

◉ to kick the bucket

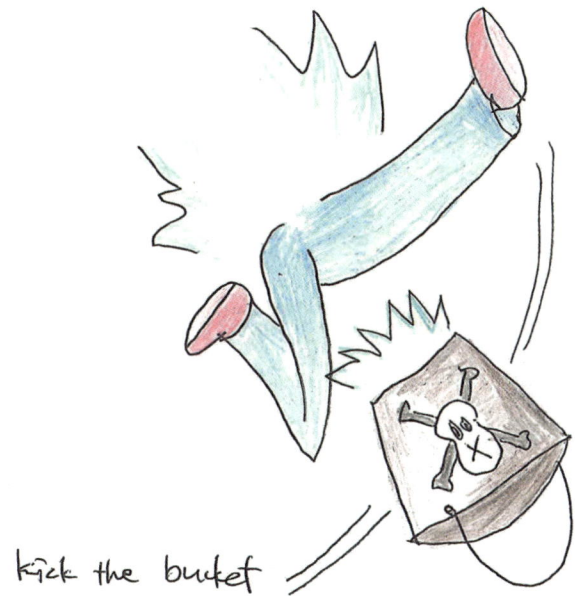

- Guess the meaning of the idiom in the dialogue below.

Ben: Did you hear Tom suddenly **kicked** the bucket?

Suzie: What happened?

Ben: Rumor says he got hit by a car.

Suzie: Oh, sorry to hear that!

L.M(표면적 의미)	F.M(비유적 의미)
양동이를 걷어차다	to die; 죽다 * bucket list: 죽기 전에 하고 싶은 일을 정리한 리스트

- History: 뒤집은 양동이 위에 서서 목을 맨 뒤, 양동이를 걷어차는 흔히 사용되었던 자살의 방법에서 유래함.

♣ Make your own dialogue.

⊙ to kill (someone) with kindness

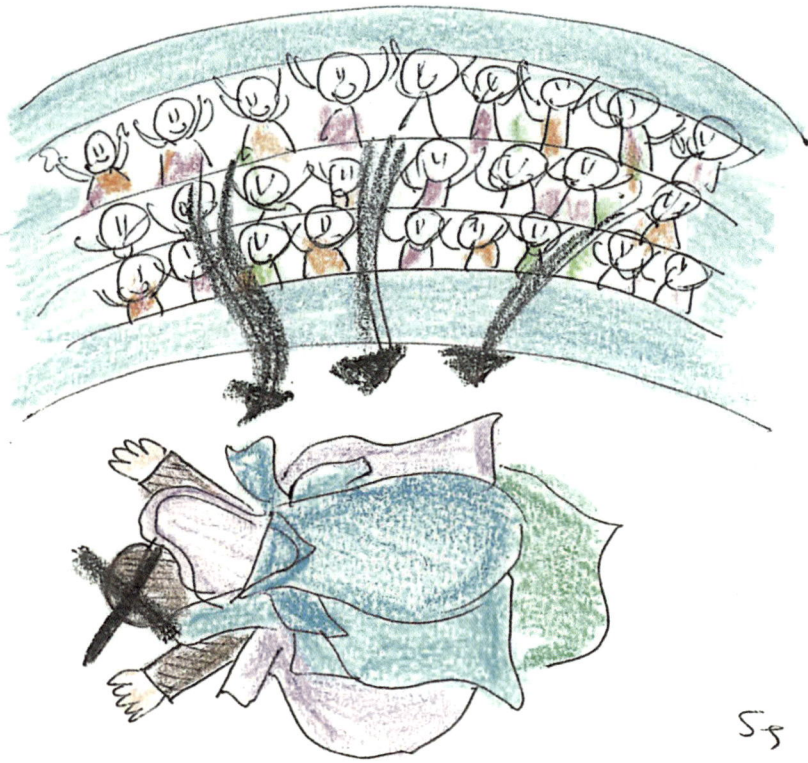

– Guess the meaning of the idiom in the dialogue below.

Ben: I think Sam is a womanizer.

Suzie: He is not. Maybe he is too kind to girls. He kills them with kindness.

L.M(표면적 의미)	F.M(비유적 의미)
누군가를 친절함으로 죽이다	to spoil or harm with well-intentioned but excessive kindess: 친절이 지나쳐 도리어 화를 입히다

– History: 1. 당시 아테네에는 헌사의 표현으로 무대로 망토를 던지는 풍습이 있었다고 함. 아테네 사람이었던 법률가인 Draco는 많은 사람들로부터 사랑을 받고 있었는데, Aegina(아이기나) 극장에 참석했을 때 많은 사람들이 그에게 헌사하기 위해 망토를 던졌음. 던져진 수많은 망토들로 인해 숨이 막혀 죽게 되었다는 데에서 유래함.

2. 또 다른 유래는 암컷 유인원이 종종 자신의 새끼를 너무 사랑한 나머지 새끼를 너무 세게 껴안아 버려 새끼가 질식했다는 설도 있음.

현재는 팝송 제목이나 컵, 티셔츠 등의 문구로도 많이 쓰이고 있음.

♣ Make your own dialogue.

⊙ (till) **Kingdom** come

– Guess the meaning of the idiom in the dialogue below.

Ben: I will love my girlfriend till *Kingdom* come.

Suzie: Wow, you are easily lovestruck. It has been only 3 days since you met her.

L.M(표면적 의미)	F.M(비유적 의미)
왕국이 올 때까지	the next life, forever, until death; 다음 생, 영원히, 죽을 때까지

– History: 성경에서 예수님의 재림, 즉 예수님이 이 세상에 하나님의 왕국을 세우는 그때까지를 의미한다고 함.

♣ Make your own dialogue.

⊙ the kiss of death

- Guess the meaning of the idiom in the dialogue below.

Ben: Sam is broke since he spent too much money on cruise trips around the world.

Suzie: They turned out to be <u>the *kiss* of death.</u>

L.M(표면적 의미)	F.M(비유적 의미)
죽음의 키스	an apparently helpful gesture but actually brings failure or ruin; 겉으로 드러난 것은 도움을 주는 행동이나 실제로는 실패나 파멸을 가져오는 것(종국에는 파멸을 가져오는 행위)

- History: 유다가 예수님에게 키스함으로써 군사들이 예수님이 누구인지 알도록 했다는 유다의 배신에 관한 성경의 글귀에서 유래함.

♣ Make your own dialogue.

◎ everything but the kitchen sink

- Guess the meaning of the idiom in the dialogue below.

Ben: Sam ordered <u>everything but the **kitchen** sink</u> when we ate out dinner.

Suzie: Did you buy him a dinner?

Ben: Yeah.

Suzie: He does that, especially when other people pay for it.

L.M(표면적 의미)	F.M(비유적 의미)
싱크대를 제외한 모든 것	absolutely everything; 실질적인 모든 것

- History: Eric Patridge가 쓴 군대의 속어/은어 사전에서 나온 말로, kitchen sink는 격렬한 집중 포격을 강조하는 말로 쓰였다고 함. 군인들은 적군이 kitchen sink를 제외한 모든 것을 다 폭격해 왔다고 표현했다고 함. 최근에는 다양한 문맥 속에서 응용되어 사용되고 있음.

♣ Make your own dialogue.

♦ knee-high to a grasshopper

- Guess the meaning of the idiom in the dialogue below.

Ben: Look at these kids. How adorable!

Suzie: They are **knee-high** to a grasshopper. I used to be like them. Those days are gone!

L.M(표면적 의미)	F.M(비유적 의미)
메뚜기만 한 무릎 높이	very small(and young); 매우 작고 어린

- History: 19세기 초반 미국에서 유래한 표현으로, 어린아이들을 무릎 높이의 작은 것들과 비교하는 데에서 시작됨. 메뚜기 이외에도 두꺼비, 개구리, 모기, 무당벌레, 새끼 오리 등이 쓰이기도 함.

♣ Make your own dialogue.

⊙ to knuckle under

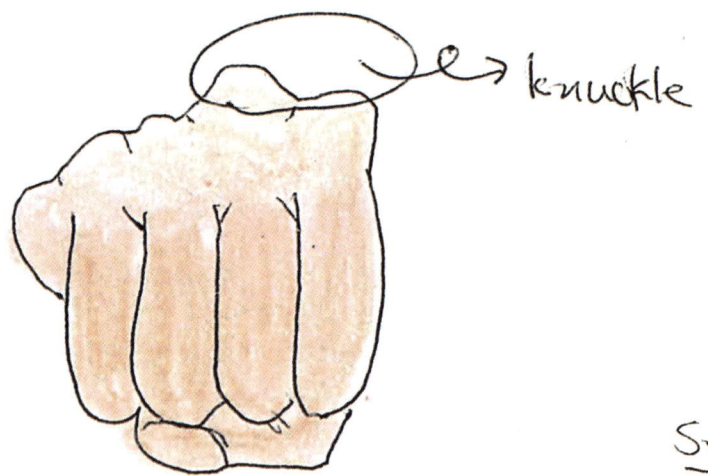

− Guess the meaning of the idiom in the dialogue below.

Ben: A new P.E. teacher looks very charismatic.

Suzie: Students seem to _knuckle under_ to his rules in class.

L.M(표면적 의미)	F.M(비유적 의미)
손가락 관절 아래	to give in, to comply; 항복하다, 순응/준수하다

− History: knuckle은 관절이나 마디를 뜻하는 말로, 꾸부리면 동그랗게 튀어나오는 부분을 말함.

♣ Make your own dialogue.

Idioms from A to Z: L

-L-

♣ These are the List of Idioms K. Are there any idioms you already know? If not, try to guess the meaning of the idioms below.

- in the **lap** of the gods ───────────────── ☐
- to **lay** it on thick / to **lay** it on with a trowel ────── ☐
- **last**-ditch ──────────────────────── ☐
- to turn over a new **leaf** ─────────────── ☐
- to pull someone's **leg** ──────────────── ☐
- a **leap** in the dark ────────────────── ☐
- to show a **leg** ─────────────────── ☐
- in the **limelight** ───────────────── ☐
- **long** in the tooth ──────────────── ☐
- a **loose** cannon ───────────────── ☐
- to **leave** someone in the **lurch** ─────────── ☐

◉ in the lap of the gods

- Guess the meaning of the idiom in the dialogue below.

Ben: How was your test yesterday?

Suzie: I did my best. Everything is in the lap of the gods now. Wish me luck!

L.M(표면적 의미)	F.M(비유적 의미)
신의 무릎 안에	the unknown outcome will be revealed in the future; 결과가 신의 소관인, 결과는 하늘에 맡긴다

- History: 고대부터 신의 형상을 한 조각상의 무릎 위에 선물을 두고 가면 기도에 대한 답변을 들을 것이라는 믿음에서 유래함.

♣ Make your own dialogue.

◉ to lay it on thick / to lay it on with a trowel

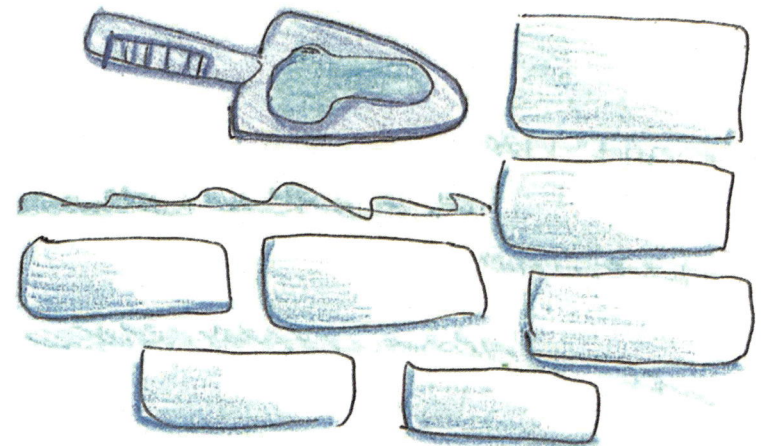

- Guess the meaning of the idiom in the dialogue below.

Ben: How was the interview for the audition?

Suzie: I tried to *lay it on thick* about myself to make a good first impression to interviewers.

L.M(표면적 의미)	F.M(비유적 의미)
모종삽으로 회반죽을 바르다	to exaggerate in order to impress, to flatter excessively: 과장하다

- History: thick은 mortar(회반죽)을 의미하고, trowel(모종삽)으로 벽돌 사이에 바르는 행위에서 유래함. 모종삽 위에 회반죽을 잘 발라서 꾸민다는 데에서 유래함.

♣ Make your own dialogue.

⊙ last-ditch

- Guess the meaning of the idiom in the dialogue below.

Ben: The Korean soccer team lost a game by a big margin against the German team.

Suzie: I know. But I highly value the attitudes of the Korean players. Even though there was a big ability gap between the teams, they did their best to the _last_ ditch.

L.M(표면적 의미)	F.M(비유적 의미)
마지막 참호	used of a final last-minute effort to avoid defeat or disaster; 마지막 방어 장소

- History: last-ditch는 마지막 전선에 있는 참호를 뜻하는데, 군대에서 패배를 피하고자 최후의 필사적인 노력을 하는 장소에서 유래함.

♣ Make your own dialogue.

Idioms from A to Z: L

⊙ to turn over a new leaf

- Guess the meaning of the idiom in the dialogue below.

Ben: He started as a barista today.

Suzie: He has courage to quit his job to turn over a new leaf.

L.M(표면적 의미)	F.M(비유적 의미)
새로운 잎(장)을 넘기다	to make a fresh start, to resolve to change one's ways for the better; 새롭게 출발하다/새사람이 되다.

- History: 나무의 잎보다는 책의 페이지를 뜻하는데, John Heywood가 쓴 글귀에서 유래함. 책을 쓰다가 의문이 드는 부분은 책장을 넘기며, 단어들을 지워 보고 다시 깨끗한 종이에 다시 써 나간다는 데에서 유래함.

♣ Make your own dialogue.

⊙ to pull someone's <u>leg</u>

- Guess the meaning of the idiom in the dialogue below.

Ben: Sam is always joking about my face.

Suzie: I felt that way, too. I don't like his way of <u>pulling my leg</u>.

L.M(표면적 의미)	F.M(비유적 의미)
누군가의 다리를 잡아당기다	to make someone the target of a good humorous joke or deception; 속이다, 놀리다, 조롱하다

- History: 19세기 후반에 형벌의 한 방법으로 사람을 매달았는데, 야외 화장실을 이용하여 그 형벌을 행할 때 사형수의 죽음이 더 빨랐다고 함. 게다가 그 사람의 아래에서 다리를 잡아당기는 행위는 그 사람을 넘어뜨림으로써 대중들에게 조롱거리의 대상으로도 만들었다는 유래가 있음

♣ Make your own dialogue.

⊙ a leap in the dark

– Guess the meaning of the idiom in the dialogue below.

Ben: He quit his job for his dream to be an actor.

Suzie: Wasn't his job stable? Hope his challenge won't ended up as a *leap* in the dark.

L.M(표면적 의미)	F.M(비유적 의미)
어둠 속에서의 도약	a step of faith, a venture whose outcome cannot be predicted; 무모한 짓

– History: 영국의 철학자인 Thomas Hobbes가 은퇴를 하면서 했던 말인 "Now I am about to take my last voyage, a great *leap in the dark*."에서 유래함. 그 이후로 많은 사람들에 의해서 사용됐는데, Sir John Vangrugh는 그의 연극에서 이 이디엄을 결혼에 비유하여 쓴 것이 유명해짐. (지금 나는 Hobbes가 말한 무모한 여정을 떠나려 한다. 결혼이란, 마치 죽음처럼 또 다른 미지의 세계와 같다. – "Now I am for Hobbes's voyage, a great *leap in the dark*. Marrige, it seems, is the other great unknown like death.")

♣ Make your own dialogue.

Idioms from A to Z: L

⊙ to show a leg

— Guess the meaning of the idiom in the dialogue below.

Ben: The musical is about to start!

Suzie: Let's show a *leg* not to be late!

L.M(표면적 의미)	F.M(비유적 의미)
다리를 보여 주다	to get up, get moving; 잠자리에서 일어나다, 급히 서두르다

— History: 19세기 중반에 배가 항구에 정박해 있는 동안, 선원들을 위문하기 위해서 여성들이 배에 탑승하는 것이 허락되었는데, 위문을 오는 여성들이 아침에 다리를 보여 주는 퍼포먼스를 한다는 연락이 오면 선원들이 활기를 띠며 일어났다는 데에서 유래함.

♣ Make your own dialogue.

◉ in the **limelight**

- Guess the meaning of the idiom in the dialogue below.

Ben: I went to a BTS concert. It was awesome.
Suzie: BTS are always in the **limelight**. I'm so jelly.

L.M(표면적 의미)	F.M(비유적 의미)
각광, 세상의 이목 안에서	in the public-eye, the center of attention; 각광을 받고, 주목을 끌고

- History: 1825년에 Thomas Drummond는 Drummond light을 발명하였는데, 실린더 안에 산화 칼슘이나 라임을 넣어서 데워진 공기로 밝은 빛을 발하는 것이었다는 데에서 유래함. 나중에 이 조명은 스포트라이트를 받는 곳인 극장, 등대 등에서 많이 사용되었다고 함.

♣ Make your own dialogue.

◎ long in the tooth

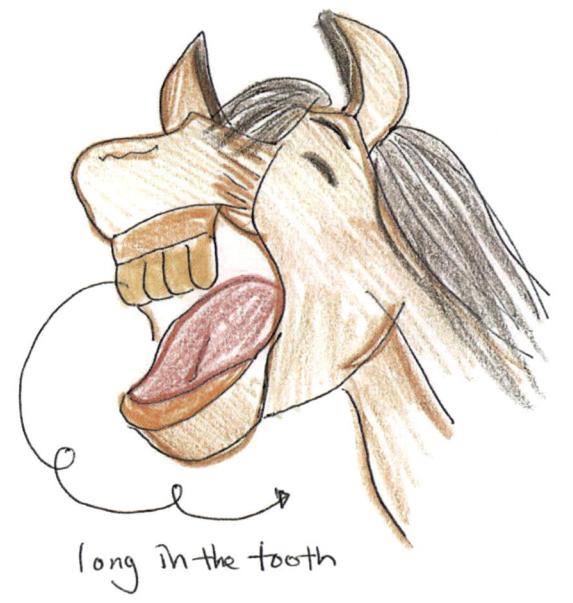

- Guess the meaning of the idiom in the dialogue below.

Ben: My teacher is **long in the tooth**, but she is still very energetic and passionate about teaching.

Suzie: Age doesn't seem to matter to her. That's why I admire her.

L.M(표면적 의미)	F.M(비유적 의미)
치아가 긴	old; 나이 든

- History: 말의 입을 보면 그 동물의 나이를 가늠할 수 있는데, 나이가 들수록 잇몸이 닳아서 이빨이 길어 보인다는 데에서 유래함.

♣ Make your own dialogue.

⊙ a loose cannon

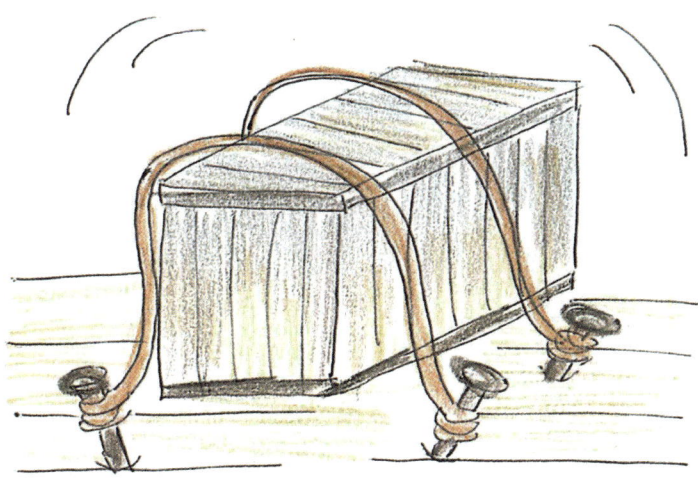

- Guess the meaning of the idiom in the dialogue below.

Ben: Tom went out of the room during the middle of the meeting out of the blue.

Suzie: He is such a *loose* cannon. I don't understand his behavior sometimes.

L.M(표면적 의미)	F.M(비유적 의미)
느슨한 대포차	someone who behaves unpredictably, often with damaging results; 종종 사고를 일으키는 예측 불허의 행동을 하는 사람

- History: 14세기에 총기류를 운반할 때, 배의 하부에 총기류를 포차에 실어서 이동하였는데, 위험하기 때문에 말뚝을 박아서 잘 고정했었야 했음. 때로 대포차가 헐겁게 고정되면 거기에 들어 있던 대포(기관포)가 위험하게 움직였다고 하는 데에서 유래함.

♣ Make your own dialogue.

⊙ to leave someone in the lurch

to leave someone in the lurch

- Guess the meaning of the idiom in the dialogue below.

Ben: I heard William is having in trouble of doing his school project.

Suzie: Maybe it is too tough for him to do it by himself.

Ben: It seems so. What about helping him out? As his bff, I can't <u>leave</u> him in <u>the lurch</u> anymore.

Suzie: Sounds good~

L.M(표면적 의미)	F.M(비유적 의미)
보드게임판(lurch)에 누군가를 남겨 두다(머물게 하다)	to abandon (a friend) to a difficult situation; 어려운 상황(곤경)에 있는 친구를 못 본 체하다/친구를 저버리다

- History:

프랑스의 주사위 놀이 게임인 Lourche에서 유래하여 영어에서는 lurch로 쓰임. Cribbage 카드 게임에서 주사위로 말을 던져 보드판에서 움직이며 자신의 카드와 상대방의 카드를 받고 버리며 계산을 하는데, 먼저 121점을 획득한 사람이 이기는 게임임. 자신이 크게 이기고 있고 상대편은 훨씬 낮은 점수의 보드판에 머물러 있는 상황을 말하는 데에서 유래함.

♣ Make your own dialogue.

Idioms from A to Z: M

-M-

♣ These are the List of Idioms M. Are there any idioms you already know? If not, try to guess the meaning of the idioms below.

- the real **McCoy** -- ☐
- as **mad** as a **March** hare ------------------------------ ☐
- to **make** (both) ends **meet** ---------------------------- ☐
- **Man** /Girl Friday -- ☐
- **man** in the street --------------------------------------- ☐
- tell it to the **marines** ---------------------------------- ☐
- There is a **method** in one's **madness** ------------------ ☐
- the **Midas** touch --- ☐
- to **mind** one's Ps and Qs --------------------------------- ☐
- once in a blue **moon** ------------------------------------- ☐

- to make a **mountain** out of a **molehill** ----------------- ☐
- cut the **mustard** ----------------------------------- ☐
- **mutton** dressed as lamb ---------------------------- ☐

◎ **the real McCoy**

- Guess the meaning of the idiom in the dialogue below.

Ben: I'm looking for tasty kimchi. Do you have any information to give me?

Suzie: Did you try the one sold in the Blue House restaurant on the corner?

Ben: Not yet.

Suzie: You should try it. The kimchi I ate there was the best. It's <u>the real McCoy</u>.

L.M(표면적 의미)	F.M(비유적 의미)
진짜 McCoy인	the authentic, ge nuine, the real thing; 진짜의

- History: 1) 20세기의 미국의 유명했던 McCoy라는 꼬마 복서와 술 취한 사람과 시비가 붙었는데, 화가 난 꼬마가 주먹을 날리자, 맞은 사람이 "너는 진짜구나"라고 말한 데에서 유래함. 2) 금주령이 내려졌던 시기에 캐나다에서 미국으로 몰래 술을 들여왔었는데, 악명 높은 밀수업자(bootlegger)였던 William Bill McCoy라는 사람이 있었고, 술에 그의 이름인 McCoy라는 이름이 붙으면 진짜 술로 인정받았다는 데에서 유래함.

♣ Make your own dialogue.

⊙ as mad as a March hare

as mad as a March hare

- Guess the meaning of the idiom in the dialogue below.

Ben: What was William upset about? He was <u>as *mad* as a *March* hare.</u>
Suzie: He dropped his new phone on the ground, and it was totally smashed.

L.M(표면적 의미)	F.M(비유적 의미)
3월의 (발정 난) 토끼처럼 미친	crazy; 미친

- History: 토끼는 예로부터 mad(미친) 성격으로 많이 비유되는데, 이는 특히 토끼가 짝짓기를 할 때 수컷이 암컷을 따라다니다가 마음에 드는 암컷을 찾으면 짝짓기 전에 때리는(boxing) 미친 행위를 한 데에서 유래한 것으로 보임. 원래 marsh hare(rabbit)였던 것이 march hare로 변질되었음.

♣ Make your own dialogue.

⊙ to make (both) ends meet

to make (both) ends meet   ss

- Guess the meaning of the idiom in the dialogue below.

Ben: Let's eat out for dinner. There is a good restaurant that has just newly opened.

Suzie: I'm afraid, but I can't. I already spent too much money this month, so I have to save money to make ends meet for the rest of this month.

Ben: Don't worry. It's on the house.

L.M(표면적 의미)	F.M(비유적 의미)
양쪽 끝을 맞추다	to live within one's means; 수지를 맞추다

- History: 회계 업무에서 유래한 것으로, 월말이나 연말에 수입과 지출을 잘 맞추는 작업을 했다는 데에서 유래함.

♣ Make your own dialogue.

◉ Man /Girl Friday

– Guess the meaning of the idiom in the dialogue below.

Suzie: How is it possible to work in the same company twenty years in a row?
Ben: Maybe I am **Man** Friday in my company?

L.M(표면적 의미)	F.M(비유적 의미)
금요일의 남자/소녀(여자)	an efficient and valued personal assistant or helper; 유능한 비서, 실력이 좋은 보조

– History: Daniel Defoe가 쓴 *Robinson Crusoe*에서 유래함. 난파선에서 홀로 외롭게 섬에서 생존해 오던 크루소는 어느 날 자신의 죄수들을 잡아먹기 위해서 섬으로 온 야만인을 놀라게 해서 쫓아내고 희생자 중의 한 명을 살려냈는데, 이 남자를 'Man Friday'라고 불렀다고 함. Man은 하인(servant)을 의미하고, Friday는 크루소가 그 남자와 처음 만났던 날을 뜻함. 후에는 여자 비서라는 말로 'Girl Friday'가 사용되기도 함.

♣ Make your own dialogue.

⊙ man in the street

- Guess the meaning of the idiom in the dialogue below.

Ben: How did the blind date go?

Suzie: I don't know yet. Maybe I have to see him a couple more times to get to know him better.

Ben: Didn't you get any good impression about him at first sight?

Suzie: Nothing special. He is just a *man* in the street.

L.M(표면적 의미)	F.M(비유적 의미)
길거리에 (있는) 남자(사람)	the average, ordinary person; 평범한 사람, 일반인

- History: 산업 혁명으로 인해, 도시의 인구는 증가했고, 예전보다 더 많은 사람들이 거리로 쏟아져 나왔다는 데에서 유래함.

♣ Make your own dialogue.

⊙ tell it to the marines

- Guess the meaning of the idiom in the dialogue below.

Ben: I got a business card from a famous entertainment agent today. He tried to cast me on the street.

Suzie: Tell it to the *marines*!

L.M(표면적 의미)	F.M(비유적 의미)
그것을 해군들에게 말하다 (이야기하다)	a remark expressing incredulity at a story; 못미더운 말을 들을 때 비꼬는 말/해병대한테나 말하시죠?

- History: 영국의 찰스 2세는 파티에서 자신이 해군에 있었을 때의 이야기를 많이 했었는데, 그중에 날아다니는 물고기 이야기를 했음. 군중들은 미덥지 않은 듯이 그를 쳐다보았는데, 함께 있었던 해군이 자신도 그것을 본 것 같다고 보태어 말하여 사람들이 찰스의 이야기를 믿게 되었다는 데에서 유래함.

♣ Make your own dialogue.

⊙ There is a **method** in one's **madness**

- Guess the meaning of the idiom in the dialogue below.

Ben: One of my classmates suddenly jumped up and down in the middle of class.
Suzie: Should <u>there be a ***method*** in his ***madness***?</u>

L.M(표면적 의미)	F.M(비유적 의미)
누군가의 미친 행동(광기)에도 조리가 있다	There is a sound reason behind apparently illogical behavior; 겉으로 드러나는 비논리적/비상식적인 행동에도 다 이유가 있다/미친 행동에도 조리가 있다

- History: 셰익스피어가 햄릿과 폴로니우스의 대사에서 왕자의 거짓 미치광이 행세에 대한 언급으로 처음 사용하였고, 그 이후 Edgar Allen Poe같은 유명 작가들도 많이 인용하여서 사용함.

♣ Make your own dialogue.

⊙ the Midas touch

the Midas Touch

— Guess the meaning of the idiom in the dialogue below.

Ben: William made a fortune from the stocks he recently invested.

Suzie: Again? He must have <u>the *Midas* touch</u>. Every time he invests in something, he makes a mint. I want to know his secret.

L.M(표면적 의미)	F.M(비유적 의미)
미다스의 손길	the ability to make money; 성공/부를 부르는 능력

— History: Bacchus을 도와준 대가로 소원을 빌게 된 Midas가 만지는 것마다 금으로 변하게 해 달라고 빌었다는 데에서 유래함.

♣ Make your own dialogue.

Idioms from A to Z: M

⊙ to mind one's Ps and Qs

- Guess the meaning of the idiom in the dialogue below.

Ben: My new boss is too sensitive about everything.
Suzie: I think he is hot-tempered. Anyway, we better *mind our* Ps and Qs when we are with him.

L.M(표면적 의미)	F.M(비유적 의미)
P와 Q에 신경을 쓰다	to take great care how one speaks, be on one's best behavior; 언행을 조심하다/신경 쓰다

- History: 1) 프랑스의 실력 있는 무용가가 제자를 가르칠 때, 제자들에게 끊임없이 pieds와 queues의 동작에 신경을 써야 한다고 상기시킨 데에서 유래함.
2) 선술집에서 손님이 술을 주문할 때 pint인지 quart인지를 정확하게 썼어야 했다는 데에서 유래.

♣ Make your own dialogue.

⊙ once in a blue **moon**

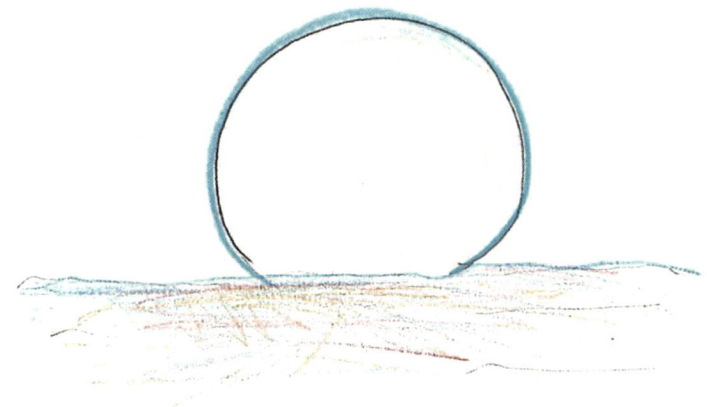

once in a blue moon   SS

- Guess the meaning of the idiom in the dialogue below.

Ben: Sam bought me a dinner yesterday.
Suzie: Wow, That happens <u>once in a blue **moon**</u>!

L.M(표면적 의미)	F.M(비유적 의미)
푸른 달이 뜨는 한 번	very rarely, hardly ever; 극히 드물게

- History: 달이 푸른빛을 띠기 위해서는 천문학적인 조건들이 갖춰져야 하는데, Krakatoa의 폭발이 발생하고, 먼지 분자가 하늘을 덮어야 가능함. 이 현상은 몇백 년 만에 한 번 생길까 말까 하는 매우 희귀한 현상이라는 데에서 유래.

♣ Make your own dialogue.

Idioms from A to Z: M

◉ to make a mountain out of a molehill

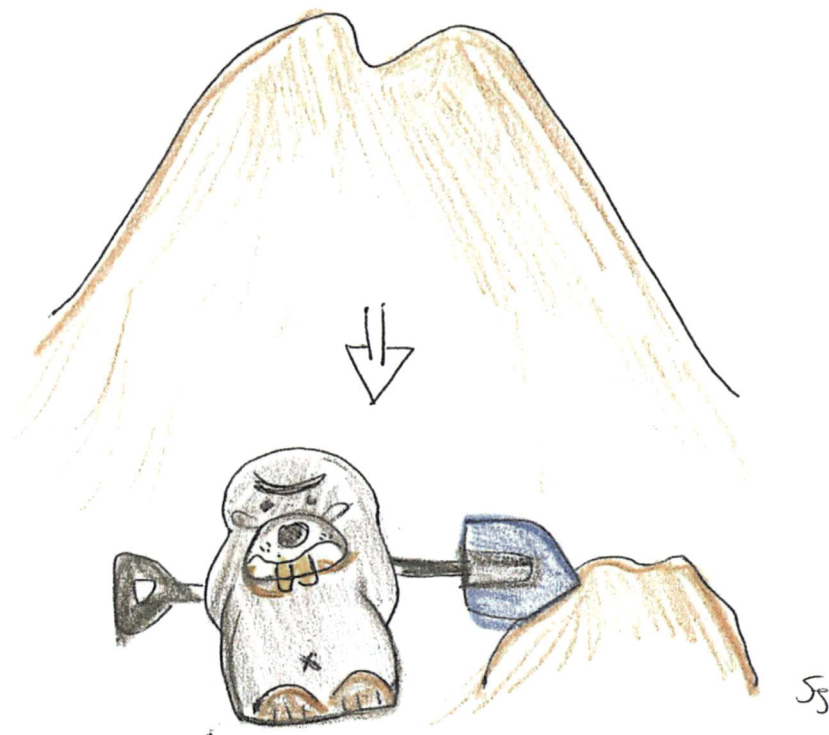

- Guess the meaning of the idiom in the dialogue below.

Ben: I heard you fell over the stairs and broke your ankle.

Suzie: No, somebody <u>made a **mountain** out of a **molehill**.</u> I missed my step from the stairs, but fortunately my ankle was just twisted. No need to worry! I already put on some pain relief patches.

L.M(표면적 의미)	F.M(비유적 의미)
두더지 둑을 산으로 만들다	to make a small problem seem much greater than it really is; 침소봉대

- History: 그리스 시대부터 사소한 것을 전혀 어울리지 않는 것에 비유한 데에서 유래함.
    ex) an elephant out of fly

♣ Make your own dialogue.

⊙ cut the mustard

cut the mustard

- Guess the meaning of the idiom in the dialogue below.

Ben: I was so shocked about my grades on the test.
Suzie: Didn't you do your best for the test?
Ben: I did, but the result won't <u>cut the **mustard**</u> to my parents' expectations.
Suzie: I think the fact that you did your best itself is important than the result.

L.M(표면적 의미)	F.M(비유적 의미)
겨자를 자르다	to come up to stardard; 기대에 부응하다

- History: O Henry가 Texas에 살았을 시절에 썼던 *The Heart of the West*라는 소설에 나왔던 글로, 음식의 맛을 좌지우지할 정도로 중요한 역할을 하는 겨자의 역할처럼 the best of anything의 의미로 사용함.

♣ Make your own dialogue.

⊙ mutton dressed as lamb

- Guess the meaning of the idiom in the dialogue below.

Suzie: How do I look?

Mom: What a short skirt!

Suzie: Mom, this is in fashion this summer. You don't know about the trend.

Mom: Think about your age! I might sound very strict, but I don't want people to consider you a *mutton* dressed as lamb.

L.M(표면적 의미)	F.M(비유적 의미)
새끼 양처럼 입은 늙은 (다 자란) 양	an older woman dressed in clothes more suited to a younger one; 어린 여자한테 어울리는 옷을 입은 나이 많은 여자

- History: mutton은 오랫동안 여성을 경멸하는 말로 빗대어서 사용되어 옴.

♣ **Make your own dialogue.**

Idioms from A to Z: N

-N-

♣ These are the List of Idioms N. Are there any idioms you already know? If not, try to guess the meaning of the idioms below.

- ⊙ a **nail** in one's coffin ──────────────────── ☐
- ⊙ (to pay) on the **nail** ──────────────────── ☐
- ⊙ in this **neck** of the woods ──────────────── ☐
- ⊙ **nectar** of the gods ──────────────────── ☐
- ⊙ a **nest** egg ────────────────────────── ☐
- ⊙ to feather one's **nest** ───────────────────── ☐
- ⊙ to grasp the **nettle** ─────────────────── ☐
- ⊙ the land of **Nod** ──────────────────── ☐
- ⊙ to pay through the **nose** ─────────────── ☐
- ⊙ to **nip** in the bud ────────────────────── ☐

◉ a **nail** in one's coffin

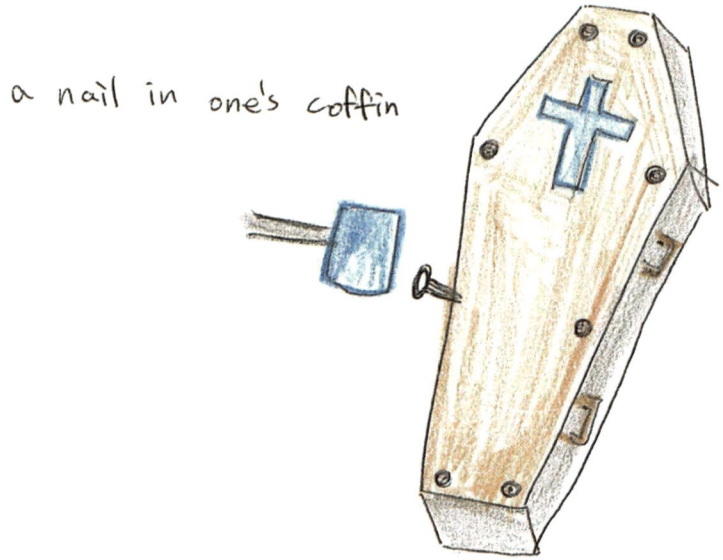

– Guess the meaning of the idiom in the dialogue below.

Ben: My dad proclaimed he would stop smoking.

Suzie: Good for him! Smoking is just <u>a *nail* in his coffin.</u>

L.M(표면적 의미)	F.M(비유적 의미)
관 속의 못	수명을 줄이는 것/실패를 초래할 결정타

– History: 19세기에 술고래들은 술을 a nail in the coffin(관 속에 못)이라고 비유하여 불렀고, 20세기에는 금연 주의자들이 coffin nail을 담배라고 부르며 "Ban the coffin nail"이라는 슬로건을 내세웠음. 담배, 심한 음주와 스트레스는 이른 사망을 초래하여 문학적으로 관 뚜껑에 못질하는 행위를 뜻하기도 함. 사용의 범위가 점점 넓어져 '실패를 초래할 결정타'라는 의미로도 사용됨.

♣ Make your own dialogue.

◉ (to pay) on the nail

- Guess the meaning of the idiom in the dialogue below.

Ben: You owe me $100.

Suzie: I know. I will <u>pay on the *nail*</u> when I get paid this month.

L.M(표면적 의미)	F.M(비유적 의미)
못 위에서 지불하다	지체 없이 즉각적으로 지불하다

- History: 영국의 서부 항구 도시인 브리스톨에서는 옥수수를 거래할 때 4개의 기둥 같은 구리로 된 못이 박혀 있던 계산대에서 흥정을 하였는데, 이 흥정은 완전히 공개된 곳에서 이루어 졌다고 함.

♣ Make your own dialogue.

⊙ in this **neck** of the woods

in this neck of the woods

- Guess the meaning of the idiom in the dialogue below.

Ben: What are you doing in this **neck** of the woods?
Suzie: I heard there is a hip cafe around here.

L.M(표면적 의미)	F.M(비유적 의미)
산림 구역에서	여기, 근처, 이웃의

- History: 17세기에는 'neck'은 좁은 구역의 땅을 의미하는 데 사용되었고, 19세기에는 'woodland settlement'는 산림 지역의 분쟁 해결에 사용됨. 20세기에 와서는 어느 위치에서든 특정한 지역이나 근처(인근)을 의미하는 것으로 넓혀져 사용됨.

♣ Make your own dialogue.

◉ **nectar of the gods**

nectar of the gods

― Guess the meaning of the idiom in the dialogue below.

Ben: Any **nectar of the gods** you can recommend for me?

Suzie: Um…. watermelon juice! Especially during summer time!

L.M(표면적 의미)	F.M(비유적 의미)
신들의 과일즙(꿀)	맛있는 음료(수)

― History: 고대 사회의 신들은 맛 좋은 음식(ambrosia)와 발효된 꿀로 만든 달콤한 음료수인 nectar(과일즙, 꿀)을 마셨다는 데에서 유래함.

♣ Make your own dialogue.

⊙ a nest egg

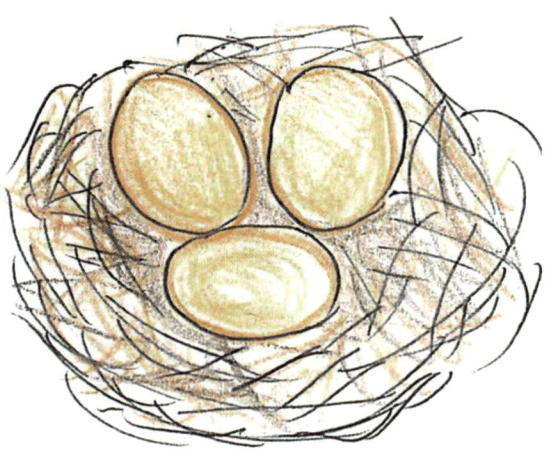

- Guess the meaning of the idiom in the dialogue below.

Ben: Recently I bought a new car.
Suzie: Wow, did you win the lottery or something?
Ben: I spent my *nest* egg for the car.

L.M(표면적 의미)	F.M(비유적 의미)
둥지에 있는 알	비상금

- History: 암탉이 더 많은 알을 낳게 하도록 알 또는 도자기로 만든 가짜 알을 둥지에 두었던 것에서 유래하여, 미래의 사용을 위해서 모아 두는 돈으로도 의미함.

♣ Make your own dialogue.

⊙ to feather one's nest

- Guess the meaning of the idiom in the dialogue below.

Ben: I love this new bag.
Suzie: Why don't you buy it?
Ben: No, I can't. I need to feather my nest.

L.M(표면적 의미)	F.M(비유적 의미)
둥지에 깃털을 대다	다른 사람의 희생을 치러서라도 자신의 부를 축적하다/채우다/ 장래에 대비하여 저축하다

- History: 새들이 자신의 둥지를 부드럽게 만들기 위해서 깃털을 안쪽에 대었다는 것에서 암시된 말로, 집을 쾌적하게 만들거나, 다른 사람의 희생을 치러서 부를 채운다는 의미로 확장되어 사용됨

♣ Make your own dialogue.

⊙ to grasp the nettle

- Guess the meaning of the idiom in the dialogue below.

Ben: I didn't get promoted this time.

Suzie: What? You deserve to be promoted. You have worked so hard.

Ben: It is so disappointing.

Suzie: Have you talked about it with your boss? You need to grasp the *nettle* sometimes.

L.M(표면적 의미)	F.M(비유적 의미)
쐐기풀을 쥐다	face a problem with determination; 선뜻 곤경에 맞서다

- History: nettle(쐐기풀)은 개미산(formic acid)와 다른 피부 자극물을 포함하는 미세한 털로 덮여 있어서 살짝만 만져도 많은 통증을 야기하는 데에서 유래함.

♣ Make your own dialogue.

⊙ the land of Nod

- Guess the meaning of the idiom in the dialogue below.

Ben: I feel so good that I took a walk this morning.
Suzie: Why didn't you take me with you?
Ben: It was at around 6 a.m. Isn't it too early for you?
Suzie: Yeah, I was in the land of *Nod* at that time. Haha.

L.M(표면적 의미)	F.M(비유적 의미)
Nod의 땅	sleep; 잠/자다

- History: 성경에서는 가인이 그의 동생인 아벨을 죽인 뒤에 그가 일했던 땅과 하나님의 존재로부터 어떻게 탈출하였는지를 말하고 있음. 가인은 Nod 땅에서 거주하였고, 조나단 스위프트가 그의 작품에서 가인의 은신처에 관한 말장난을 만들었고, 동사 'nod'는 '나른해지다', '잠이 들다'의 의미로 사용됨.

♣ Make your own dialogue.

◉ to pay through the nose

- Guess the meaning of the idiom in the dialogue below.

Ben: Finally I succeeded in getting a limited pair of sneakers.

Suzie: I love them.

Ben: Although I paid through the *nose*, it' was worth buying them.

L.M(표면적 의미)	F.M(비유적 의미)
코를 통하여(코로) 지불하다/대가를 치르다	to pay an exorbitant price for something; 바가지 쓰다/비싸게 값을 지불하다

- History: 1. 덴마크인들이 아일랜드의 침입에 성공하였을 때, 아일랜드인에게 엄청난 세금을 부과 하였는데, 세금을 내지 않는 사람들의 코를 베어서(slit) 고통을 받게 하는 벌을 주었다 는 데에서 유래함.

    2. 또는 Rhino(코뿔소)는 '돈'과 '코'를 둘 다 의미하였고, 'to bleed'는 '엄청난 돈을 잃다'를 의 미하여 'noses bleed'라는 의미는 'to pay through the nose'라는 뜻으로 사용되기도 함.

♣ Make your own dialogue.

Idioms from A to Z: N

⊙ to nip in the bud

- Guess the meaning of the idiom in the dialogue below.

Ben: Saera got an F on her final essay. It is said that she got caught plagiarizing on her essay.

Suzie: Plagiarizing is cheating. It would make sense for school teachers to <u>nip in the bud</u> any tendency of students to plagiarize.

Ben: You can say that again!

L.M(표면적 의미)	F.M(비유적 의미)
봉오리의 한 부분을 잘라내다	초기에 싹을 없애다/미연에 방지하다

- History: 봉오리나 나뭇가지 줄기를 잘라 냄으로써 초기에 성장이 방해/지연될 수 있는 것을 방지한다는 데에서 유래함.

♣ Make your own dialogue.

Idioms from A to Z: O

-O-

♣ These are the List of Idioms O. Are there any idioms you already know? If not, try to guess the meaning of the idioms below.

- ◉ in the **offing** -- ☐
- ◉ to **over-egg** the pudding ------------------------------ ☐
- ◉ to pour **oil** on troubled waters ------------------------ ☐
- ◉ to go **over** the top --- ☐

⊙ in the offing

- Guess the meaning of the idiom in the dialogue below.

Ben: How is the preparation going for your wedding? It is <u>in the **offing**</u>, right?
Suzie: So far, so good. I'm nervous, though.
Ben: Try to think about your bright future with your husband-to-be.

L.M(표면적 의미)	F.M(비유적 의미)
바다의 가장 먼 부분	very likely to happen, imminent; 머지않아

- History: 16세기에는 offing이 육지에서 보이지만 바다의 가장 먼 부분의 지리적인 거리를 감안한 '아주 먼 미래'를 뜻하였으나, 이러한 개념은 19세기에 사라져 해안에서 감별되는 어떤 선박은 전체 바다에 비하여 '그다지 멀리 있지 않다'는 의미가 시간적 개념에도 사용됨.

♣ Make your own dialogue.

⊙ to over-egg the pudding

- Guess the meaning of the idiom in the dialogue below.

Ben: Let's decide where to go for a school trip.

Suzie: I agree with you. We have discussed it too long. It's not good to **over-egg** the pudding.

L.M(표면적 의미)	F.M(비유적 의미)
푸딩에 달걀을 너무 많이 풀다	to exaggerate grossly, to spoil something by going much too far; 한 문제를 너무 많이 논의하다, 사족을 달다

- History: 푸딩을 만드는 데 너무 많은 달걀을 넣으면 반죽을 망친다는 데에서 유래함.

♣ Make your own dialogue.

⦿ to pour oil on troubled waters

- Guess the meaning of the idiom in the dialogue below.

Ben: Did you make up with Sam?

Suzie: Yes, I tried my best to <u>pour *oil* on troubled waters</u>.

L.M(표면적 의미)	F.M(비유적 의미)
소용돌이치는 물 안에 기름을 붓다	to soothe a quarrel, to calm a hearted argument; 분쟁을 가라앉히다, 노여움을 달래다

- History: Aidan 주교의 기적 이야기에서 유래함. Utta라 불리던 신부가 Osway 왕의 신부를 바다 건너 모시고 갈 일이 있었는데, 떠나기 전에 Aidan 주교를 만나게 되었고 주교는 Utta 신부에게 성스러운 기름 한 병을 주면서 바다에서 큰 풍랑을 만나게 될 것이지만 이 기름을 뿌려 주면 파도는 잔잔해질 것이라고 예언함. 실제로 바다에 큰 폭풍이 몰아닥쳤는데, Aidan 주교의 예언을 기억했던 Utta 신부는 기름을 바다에 뿌렸고, 그러자 바다는 잔잔해졌다고 함.

♣ Make your own dialogue.

⊙ to go over the top

− Guess the meaning of the idiom in the dialogue below.

Ben: I was upset about Sam.

Suzie: What for?

Ben: I made a tiny mistake when Sam and I presented my group project.

Suzie: And?

Ben: After the presentation, he blamed me a lot for my mistake.

Suzie: He is too competitive. I guess he went **over** the top again.

L.M(표면적 의미)	F.M(비유적 의미)
정상 위로 올라가다	to go too far, to behave immoderately; 돌격하다, 한도를 넘어서다, 과하게 몰입하다

− History: 1차 세계 대전의 참호전에서 유래함. 공격을 개시하기 위해서, 군인들은 먼저 동맹군과 적군 사이의 어느 누구도 차지하지 않은 영역에 뛰어들기 전에 참호의 난간 위를 올라타는 매우 위험한 행동을 해야 했다는 데에서 유래함.

♣ **Make your own dialogue.**

Idioms from A to Z: P

-P-

♣ These are the List of Idioms P. Are there any idioms you already know? If not, try to guess the meaning of the idioms below.

- ⊙ to **paddle** one's own canoe ☐
- ⊙ to **paint** the town red ☐
- ⊙ beyond the **pale** ☐
- ⊙ to **pan** out (well/badly) ☐
- ⊙ **Pandora**'s box ☐
- ⊙ a **paper** tiger ☐
- ⊙ the **pecking** order ☐
- ⊙ **pastures** new ☐
- ⊙ a round **peg** in a square/ a square in a round hole ☐
- ⊙ the **penny** dropped ☐

- in a **pickle** -- ☐
- **pie** in the sky ------------------------------------- ☐
- to buy/sell a **pig** in a **poke** -------------------- ☐
- in the **pink** -- ☐
- a **pound** of flesh ----------------------------------- ☐
- a **Pyrrhic** victory ---------------------------------- ☐
- to go to **pot** --------------------------------------- ☐

⊙ to paddle one's own canoe

- Guess the meaning of the idiom in the dialogue below.

Ben: Can you please help me out to complete this project?

Suzie: Have you tried to *paddle your own canoe* for this project?

L.M(표면적 의미)	F.M(비유적 의미)
자기 스스로 배의 노를 젓다	to be independent, to get along by one's own effrots; 독립적인, 스스로의 노력으로 살아가다

- History: 19세기 초반 미서부에서 만들어진 말로, Sarah Bolton이 쓴 영감 있는 시에서 반복적으로 사용됨으로써 일반인들의 관심을 얻게 됨. 인생이란 바다를 여행하는 자들은 자신들의 운이 어떨지라도 "Paddle your own canoes"라고 말하고 있음. "Leave to Heaven, in humble trust, All you will to do; But if you succeed, you must paddle your own canoe." ('모든 것은 겸손한 자세로 하늘에 맡겨라. 하지만 성공한다면, 스스로 노를 저어라'라고 말함.)

♣ Make your own dialogue.

Idioms from A to Z: P

⊙ to paint the town red

- Guess the meaning of the idiom in the dialogue below.

Ben: Wow, finally we are done with the final exam. Time for celebration!
Suzie: Of course, let's **paint the town red** tonight! Forget all about the exam.

L.M(표면적 의미)	F.M(비유적 의미)
마을을 빨갛게 페인트칠하다	to go out on a spree, to indulge in excessive revelry; 흥청망청 마시고 놀다

- History: 1. paint는 drink를 나타내는 slang으로, 빨간 코와 붉어진 뺨은 과음을 나타낸다고 함.
  2. 흥청거리며 노는 카우보이가 자신을 멈추려는 자들에게 총을 쏘아대며 빨간색으로 페인트칠한다고 경고한다는 데에서 유래.
  3. 빨강은 사람들이 즐거운 시간을 보낼 때 왁자지껄하고 신나는 분위기랑 일치하는 색상이라고 함.

♣ **Make your own dialogue.**

⊙ beyond the pale

- Guess the meaning of the idiom in the dialogue below.

Ben: My English teacher was very upset about Sally's attitude toward her.
Suzie: She was too rude to the teacher. Her attitude was <u>beyond the *pale*</u> for the teacher.

L.M(표면적 의미)	F.M(비유적 의미)
말뚝 넘어서	outside civilized society or limits, beyond acceptable conduct; 도리를 벗어난, 용인할 수 없는

- History: 'pale'은 라틴어 Palum에서 유래한 것으로, 목조 말뚝을 의미하였고, 나아가서 어떤 특정한 지휘자나 관할권 내의 울타리를 의미하게 됨.

♣ Make your own dialogue.

◉ **to pan out (well/badly)**

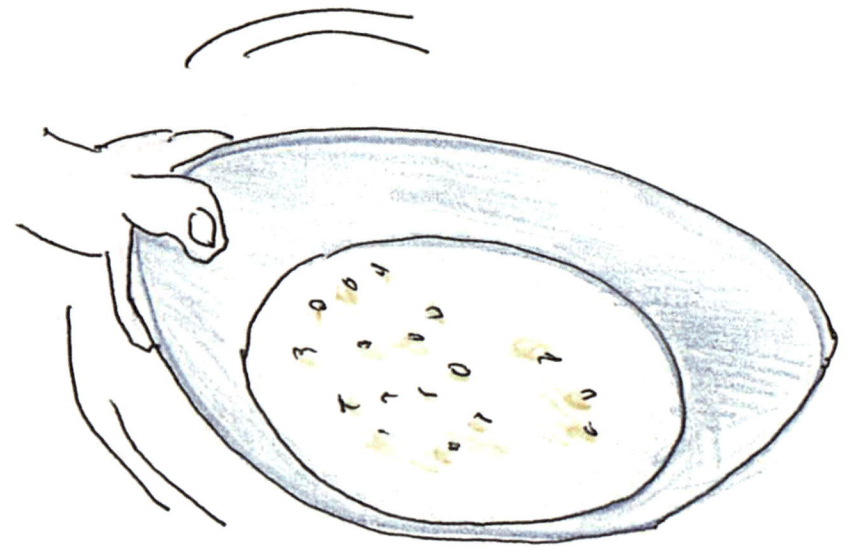

Guess the meaning of the idiom in the dialogue below.

Ben: How did the result of the audition turn out?

Suzie: It didn't *pan out well.*

Ben: Don't be too disappointed! There will be a bunch of opportunities for you.

L.M(표면적 의미)	F.M(비유적 의미)
팬을 흔들어 사금이 잘/안 나오다	여to do one's very best/worst; to work out, to turn out well/badly; 열심히 노력하고 결과가 잘 나오다/안 나오다기, 근처, 이웃의

- History: 1848년 1월 24일 James Wilson Marshall은 John Sutter의 영토에 제재소를 짓다가 금을 발견하게 되었는데, 그 뉴스는 곧 퍼져 나가서 사람들이 그 지역으로 금을 찾으러 몰려 왔다고 함. 팬에 있던 모래와 자갈을 잘 흔들어서 잘 고르면, 반짝이는 금을 발견하게 되었다는 데에서 유래함.

♣ Make your own dialogue.

Idioms from A to Z: P

◉ **Pandora's box**

- Guess the meaning of the idiom in the dialogue below.
Ben: You should be cautious with my teacher especially when he is angry.
Suzie: I know. I don't want to open *Pandora's box.*

L.M(표면적 의미)	F.M(비유적 의미)
판도라의 상자	a seemingly harmless situation fraught with hidden difficulties; 뜻하지 않은 재앙을 초래하는 것/상황

- History: 프로메테우스는 제우스신을 노하게 하였고, 그 복수로 제우스는 판도라라는 여성을 만들었는데, 프로메테우스의 동생인 에피메테우스는 첫눈에 판도라를 보고 사랑에 빠지고 맘. 둘은 결혼을 하고 제우스는 축하 선물로 상자를 보내는데, 프로메테우스는 동생에게 절대로 이 상자를 열지 말라고 경고했음. 그런데도 판도라는 호기심에 상자를 열어 버렸고, 상자 안에서부터 세상의 모든 재앙/악재들이 풀려 나왔다고 함. 상자 안 가장 바닥에 'hope'가 남겨져 있었다고 함. 이는 모든 고난과 재앙 끝에는 희망이 찾아온다는 세상의 이치를 의미하기도 함.

♣ Make your own dialogue.

◉ a paper tiger

- Guess the meaning of the idiom in the dialogue below.

Ben: The current president is about to retire.

Suzie: He must be afraid of becoming a lame duck.

Ben: Politicians and the media seem to consider him as a *paper tiger* already.

L.M(표면적 의미)	F.M(비유적 의미)
종이호랑이	a person, country or organization that in apparently powerful but actually ineffective; 실제로는 별 영향력이 없으나, 보기에는 강력해 보이는 사람, 나라 또는 조직

- History: 1946년에 미국인 기자인 Anna Louise Strong와의 인터뷰에서 Mao Tsetung(마오쩌둥)이 사용한 이후로 많이 사용하게 된 중국어 표현임. 반란군을 'a paper tiger'라고 일컬었다는 데에서 유래함

♣ Make your own dialogue.

◉ the pecking order

- Guess the meaning of the idiom in the dialogue below.

Ben: Are you at the bottom of <u>the *pecking* order</u> in your club?
Suzie: Not at the bottom. I guess I am in the middle.

L.M(표면적 의미)	F.M(비유적 의미)
쪼기 순서	a hierarchy of authority and dominance; 권위나 지배의 위계

- History: 닭장 안에서 많이 일어나는 엄격한 위계질서로 잘 알려짐. 닭장은 한 암탉에 의해서 지배되는데, 이 암탉은 다른 암탉에 쪼임을 당하지 않고, 마음대로 다른 암탉을 쪼을 수 있는 권한을 가지고 있다고 함. 다른 암탉들도 자신보다 낮은 위계의 암탉들에게 쫄 수 있었다는 데에서 유래함.

♣ Make your own dialogue.

◎ pastures new

- Guess the meaning of the idiom in the dialogue below.

Ben: Sam quit his job and started taking classes.

Suzie: Wow, It is __pastures new__ for him.

L.M(표면적 의미)	F.M(비유적 의미)
말뚝 넘어서	outside civilized society or limits, beyond acceptable conduct; 도리를 벗어난, 용인할 수 없는

- History: John Milton이 불행하게 죽은 학우를 위해 쓴 애도 시였던 *Lycidas*의 마지막 라인에 쓰였던 표현에서 유래함.

　　At last, he rose, and twitch'd his mantle *blue*;
　　Tomorrow to fresh woods, and *Pastures new*.

　　라임을 위해서 blue와 new를 맞춰 썼지만, 현대 영어에서는 new pastures로 많이 쓰이기도 함.

♣ Make your own dialogue.

Idioms from A to Z: P

⊙ a round peg in a square/ a square in a round hole

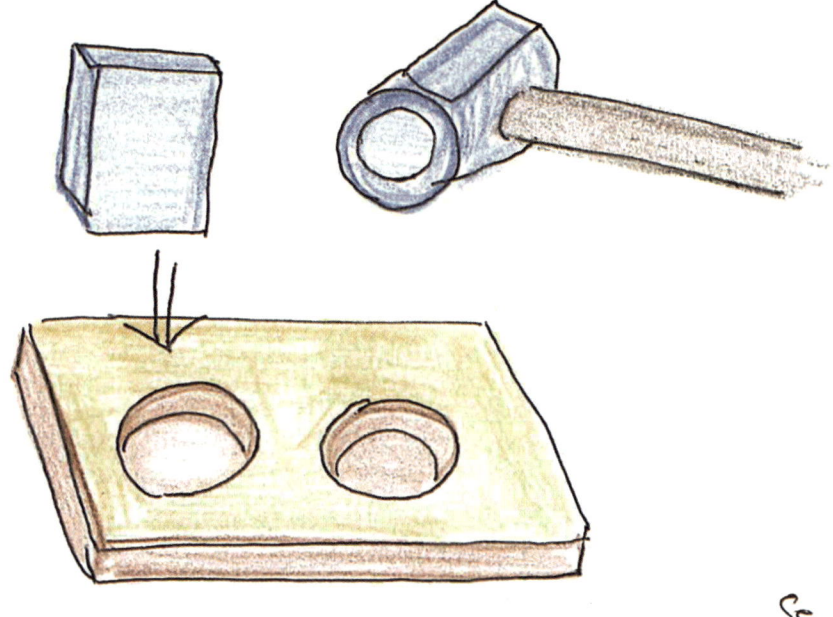

− Guess the meaning of the idiom in the dialogue below.

Ben: I have difficulty getting along with other classmates when I am doing school projects.

Suzie: You may be <u>a round *peg* in a square</u> in your group. Make more effort.

L.M(표면적 의미)	F.M(비유적 의미)
네모 구멍에 동그란 말뚝/ 동그란 구멍에 네모진 말뚝	a person whose talents or character are totally unsuited to the demands made on them; 유능하지만 부적격인

− History: 목사인 Sydney Smith가 동그란 모양의 사람은 네모 구멍에 맞지 않아서 들어가지 않는다는 것을 예시로 들며 이 사회에도 요구하는 재능이나 조건에 잘 맞지 않는 특성이나 개성을 지닌 사람들이 존재함을 꼬집어 설명함. Mark Twain도 당시 사회에서 요구하는 글의 스타일에 맞추기 위해서 많이 자신의 모양(shape)을 바꿔 나갔을 것이라 언급함.

♣ Make your own dialogue.

Idioms from A to Z: P

⊙ the penny dropped

- Guess the meaning of the idiom in the dialogue below.

Ben: I don't get my teacher's jokes.

Suzie: Almost all his jokes are from Star Wars. Why don't you watch it so that the *penny* drops?

L.M(표면적 의미)	F.M(비유적 의미)
동전이 떨어졌다	the joke, remark or point of the argument has suddenly been understood; 농담, 말, 논쟁의 포인트가 갑자기 이해됨

- History: 20세기에 동전을 넣어서 작동시켰던 slot machine에 비유된 데에서 유래함. 항구나 아케이드 쪽에 이런 기계들이 많았는데, 그 기계들은 작동하지 않다가 동전을 넣는 순간 다시 작동하기 시작한다는 이치에서 사용됨.

♣ Make your own dialogue.

◉ in a pickle

- Guess the meaning of the idiom in the dialogue below.

Ben: I lost my cellphone. Everything is in it…. What can I do?

Suzie: Gee, you must be in a pickle. Where was the last place you visited?

L.M(표면적 의미)	F.M(비유적 의미)
피클 안에	in a difficult situation, in a mess; 어려운 상황에서

- History: 중세 시대에 저염된 야채나 고기는 식단(사)의 아주 중요한 부분을 차지하였는데, 그 시대에는 신선한 식재료를 구하기 힘들었고, 식량이 부족했던 긴 겨울 동안 식재료를 구하는 것과 보관하는 것이 힘들었던 당시의 곤궁한 상황을 의미함.

♣ Make your own dialogue.

◎ **pie** in the sky

- Guess the meaning of the idiom in the dialogue below.

Ben: I want to date IU.

Suzie: In your dream! That's *pie in the sky*.

L.M(표면적 의미)	F.M(비유적 의미)
하늘에 있는 파이	heavenly rewards; an unrealistic dream, ambition, or goal; 천상의 선물, 비현실적인 꿈 또는 야망, 목표

- History: Joel Emmanuel Haggland는 스웨덴에서 가난하게 태어나 꿈을 안고 미국으로 이민을 왔으나, 미국에서의 삶도 녹록지 않았다고 함. 1910년 Joel은 Wobblies라는 세계 노동자를 위한 조합에 가입하는데, 회원들에게 작은 빨간 노래책을 나눠 주었는데, 그 노래 중의 가사 내용에 'pie in the sky'가 언급된 데에서 유래함.

　… Work and pray

　Live on hay

　You'll get *pie in the sky* when you die…

♣ **Make your own dialogue.**

⊙ to buy/sell a pig in a poke

- Guess the meaning of the idiom in the dialogue below.

Ben: I'm regretting buying this bag.
Suzie: Why did you buy it?
Ben: A sales staff wheedled me into buying it saying it looks amazing on me.
Suzie: You bought <u>a *pig* in a *poke*.</u>

L.M(표면적 의미)	F.M(비유적 의미)
작은 보따리 안에 들어있는 돼지를 사다/팔다	to buy something without inspecting it carefully first, then find it defective/to sell something off as better than it really is; 무턱대고 사다, 얼떨결에 사다, 충동구매를 하다

- History: poke는 작은 보따리(주머니)를 의미하는데, 중세 시대에는 시골 장이나 축제에서 흔했던 사기 행태가 보따리 안에 길고양이를 넣고서 돼지 새끼라고 속여서 팔았던 것임. 당한 손님은 제대로 보따리 안을 살펴보지 않고 그대로 들고 가서 결국 집에 도착해서야 사기 당했던 것을 알게 되었다는 데에서 유래함

♣ Make your own dialogue.

Idioms from A to Z: P

⊙ in the pink

- Guess the meaning of the idiom in the dialogue below.

Ben: How are you today? I heard that you felt under the weather yesterday.
Suzie: Thanks for asking me. I'm in the *pink* today.
Ben: Good to hear!

L.M(표면적 의미)	F.M(비유적 의미)
분홍색의	in the best of health; to the highest degree (of something); 최상의 (건강) 상태인

- History: 농학 전문 작가였던 Thomas Tusser은 카네이션 계열의 꽃을 pinks로 언급하였고, 다른 약초 재배자들도 그를 따라서 사용하였다는 데에서 유래함. 13세기부터 flower는 '눈에 띄는 품질의 완벽한 구현(체현)'으로 사용되었고, 나중에는 '무언가의 최상의 예시'를 나타내는 데에 쓰였음. 셰익스피어도 *Romeo and Juliet* 극본에서 Romeo와 그의 절친인 Mercutio의 유쾌한 농담 장면에서 flower을 pink로 대신하여 사용하였음.

Mercutio: "Nay, I am the very *pink* of curtesie.(명예로움)"
Romeo: "*Pinks* for flower!"

♣ **Make your own dialogue.**

⊙ a pound of flesh

- Guess the meaning of the idiom in the dialogue below.

Ben: I am in a pickle for paying back the money for a brand-new car.
Suzie: Your car is too expensive!
Ben: I know…. paying back the money is <u>a *pound* of flesh.</u>

L.M(표면적 의미)	F.M(비유적 의미)
1파운드의 살	a full, legal entitlement which one exacts out of vengeance or to the detriment of the other party; 갚는 데 엄청난 고통이 따르는 빚, 엄격한/지독한 요구

- History: 셰익스피어의 《베니스의 상인》에 나오는 Antonio와 고리대금업자였던 Shylock의 일화에서 유래하는 이디엄임. Shylock에게 빚을 갚지 못하면 자신의 살점 1파운드를 주겠다고 약속하고 돈을 빌렸던 Antonio는 결국 배가 난파되어 빚을 기한 내에 갚지 못하였고, Shylock은 Antonio에게 소송을 걸어 그의 살점을 가져가고자 하였다. 이에 변호사인 Portia는 그의 살점 1파운드를 가져가기 위해서는 1파운드의 살점 이외에 단 한 방울의 피도 흘려서는 안 된다고 주장하며 변호한 데에서 유래함.

♣ Make your own dialogue.

◉ a **Pyrrhic** victory

- Guess the meaning of the idiom in the dialogue below.

Ben: The war between Russia and Ukraine is taking a long time.
Suzie: Even if either Russia or Ukraine wins, it will end up a <u>*Pyrrhic* victory</u>.
Ben: That's what I think. The war itself is just a disaster!

L.M(표면적 의미)	F.M(비유적 의미)
Pyrrhic왕의 승리	a victory won at too great a price; 큰 희생, 이익 없는 승리

- History: Epirus왕인 야망 있는 Pyrrhus는 로마가 그리스 도시들을 위협할 때 돕겠다며 아폴로 신전의 예언자들의 격려를 받으며 이탈리아를 침입하였음. 초기 군대의 성공에도 불구하고 로마인들은 평화 제안을 거부하였고, 이에 Pyrrhus는 Apulia도 침입했어야 했음. 그는 또다시 승리를 거두기는 하였으나, 그로 인해 그의 훌륭한 군사들과 능력 있던 부하들을 많이 잃게 되어 엄청난 대가를 치렀어야 했다는 데에서 유래함.

♣ **Make your own dialogue.**

⊙ to go to **pot**

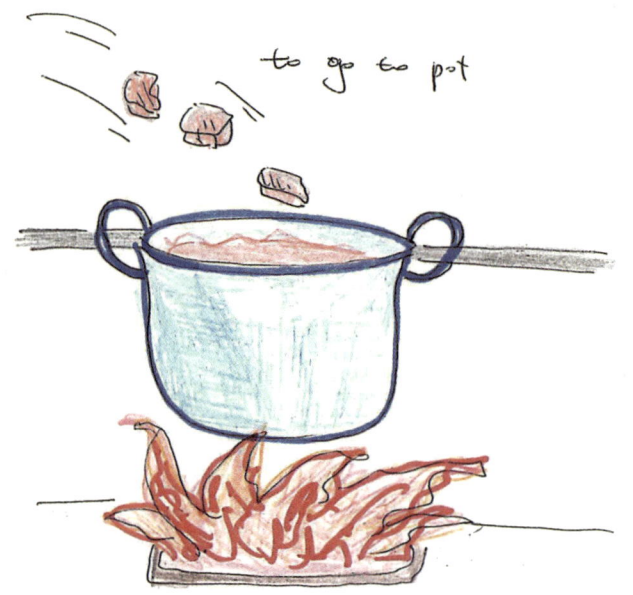

- Guess the meaning of the idiom in the dialogue below.

Ben: Julie got caught plagiarizing on her final report.
Suzie: Really? Time to <u>go to **pot**</u> for her.

L.M(표면적 의미)	F.M(비유적 의미)
냄비로 가다(냄비에 넣다)	to be ruined, to deteriorate, to go downhill; 망가진, 악화되다, 내리막길로 들어서다

- History: 16세기 초부터 사용되었던 이디엄으로, 질이 좋지 않은 고기는 잘게 잘라서 냄비 안에 넣어서 스튜 식으로 요리하는 데 사용하였는데, 이런 질이 낮은 고기 같은 존재를 가리켜 문자 그대로 '망가진' 사람을 비유하는 데에 쓰였음.

♣ Make your own dialogue.

Idioms from A to Z: Q

-Q-

♣ These are the List of Idioms Q. Are there any idioms you already know? If not, try to guess the meaning of the idioms below.

- **quantum** leap/jump ---------------------------------- ☐
- in **Queer** Street ------------------------------------ ☐
- the **quick** and the dead ----------------------------- ☐
- to **queer** someone's pitch --------------------------- ☐
- to be cut to the **quick** ----------------------------- ☐

⊙ quantum leap/jump

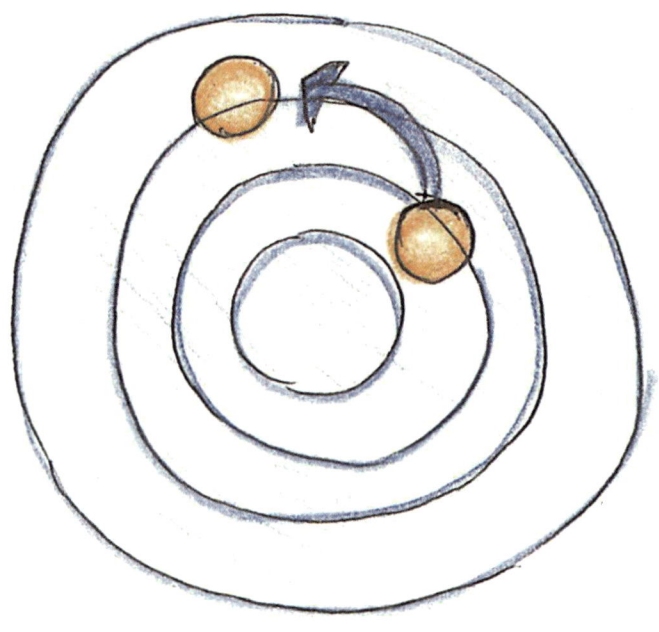

— Guess the meaning of the idiom in the dialogue below.

Suzie: I saw you play soccer yesterday.

Ben: Did you? I'm so disappointed my team didn't make it.

Suzie: Don't say that. Sometimes doing best itself is more meaningful than winning.

Ben: You think so?

Suzie: Yes. By the way, I thought you made a *quantum leap* in the game. I still remember you were on the bench for the entire game last year.

L.M(표면적 의미)	F.M(비유적 의미)
비약적인 도약/점프	a dramatic advance, a positive stride forward; 극적인 진전, 긍정적인 커다란 진전

— History: 20세기에 Planck와 Einsein이 20세기 초에 quantum(양자) 개념을 소개한 데에서 유래함. 1920년대부터, a quantum jump는 한 곳에서 다른 곳으로의 즉각적인 이동을 나타냈고, 나중에는 여러 기술적인 의미로, 많이 비유적으로 사용되었음.

♣ Make your own dialogue.

◉ in Queer Street

- Guess the meaning of the idiom in the dialogue below.

Ben: I like your new bag.

Suzie: Thanks. This is brand-new.

Ben: It must be very expensive, though.

Suzie: Yeah. Actually, I am <u>in Queer Street</u> now to pay the money back for this bag.

L.M(표면적 의미)	F.M(비유적 의미)
Queer 거리에서	in debt; 경제적 곤란

- History: Queer Street는 19세기에 병부터 실업의 경제적 걱정까지 모든 어려움으로 고통받는 사람들이 거주하던 가상의 거리를 나타냈음. London의 Carey Street의 별칭이라고도 함.

♣ Make your own dialogue.

⊙ the quick and the dead

- Guess the meaning of the idiom in the dialogue below.

Ben: The Bible says that he ascended into Heaven. From thence he shall come to judge the *quick* and the dead.

Suzie: Amen!

L.M(표면적 의미)	F.M(비유적 의미)
산 사람과 죽은 사람	the living and the dead; 산 자와 죽은 자

- History: 신약성서에서 하나님의 신판에 관해 '그는 산 자와 죽은 자(the quick and the dead)를 심판하러 오실 것이다'라고 나온 데에서 유래함.

♣ Make your own dialogue.

◎ to queer someone's pitch

- Guess the meaning of the idiom in the dialogue below.

Ben: How come you were late for the show?
Suzie: Sorry, there was a terrible traffic jam.
Ben: Anyway, you *queered* my pitch.
Suzie: I know. I feel deeply sorry.

L.M(표면적 의미)	F.M(비유적 의미)
누군가의 공연 자리를 망치다	(intentionally) to spoil someone's chances of success, to make life difficult for someone; 다른 사람의 인생을 어렵게 만들기 위해서 그의 성공 기회를 망치다

- History: 19세기에 행상인, 무역가, 공연인 사이에 흔하게 사용하였던 이디엄으로, 그들의 사업/일이 방해받았을 때 사용되었음. Thomas Frost는 그의 *Circus Life and Circus Celebrities*라는 책에서 그들의 공연을 위해 선택한 장소가 그들의 공연장(pitch)이고, 그들의 공연을 방해하는 예컨대 사고, 또는 경찰의 방해 등은 'to queer the pitch'라고 불렀음.

♣ Make your own dialogue.

Idioms from A to Z: Q

⊙ to be cut to the quick

to be cut to the quick

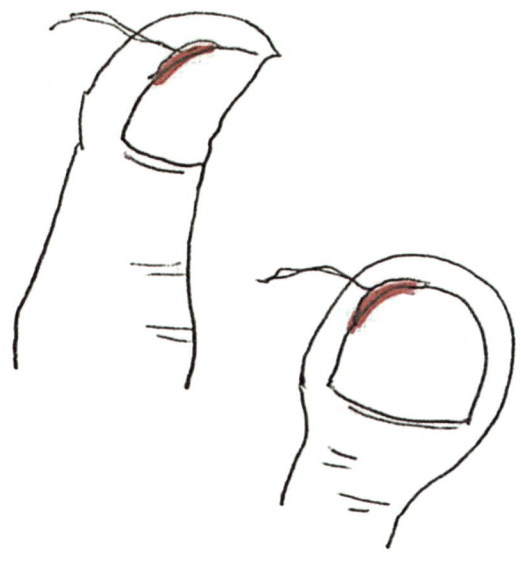

- Guess the meaning of the idiom in the dialogue below.

Ben: You look so sad!

Suzie: I broke up with my boyfriend.

Ben: I'm sorry.

Suzie: I feel like being cut to the *quick*.

L.M(표면적 의미)	F.M(비유적 의미)
가장 예민한 살점이 찢겨 나가다	to suffer deep emotional hurt; 깊은 감정적 상처로 고통받다

- History: Quick은 고대 영어에서 living(살다)의 뜻이 있었고, 손톱이나 발톱으로 보호받는 인간의 살점 중에서 가장 예민한 부위를 가리켰다고 함. 'cut to the quick'이라고 하면, 부드러운 살점이 찢겨 나간 것처럼 극심한 고통을 느낀다는 비유에서 유래함.

♣ Make your own dialogue.

Idioms from A to Z: Q

Idioms from A to Z: R

-R-

♣ These are the List of Idioms R. Are there any idioms you already know? If not, try to guess the meaning of the idioms below.

- ⊙ the three **Rs** -- ☐
- ⊙ **rack** one's brains ---------------------------------- ☐
- ⊙ to **rain** cats and dogs ---------------------------- ☐
- ⊙ in the **red** --- ☐
- ⊙ to **read** between the lines ----------------------- ☐
- ⊙ a **red** herring --------------------------------------- ☐
- ⊙ a **red**-letter day ----------------------------------- ☐
- ⊙ to **ring** a bell -------------------------------------- ☐
- ⊙ to **ride roughshod** over -------------------------- ☐
- ⊙ to **ring** true/false --------------------------------- ☐

- to know/learn the **ropes** ─────────────────────── ☐
- to sell someone down the **river** ───────────────── ☐
- between a **rock** and a hard place ──────────────── ☐
- to cry/proclaim/shout something from the **rooftops** ───── ☐
- to cross the **Rubicon** ──────────────────────── ☐
- a/the **rule** of thumb ────────────────────────── ☐

⊙ the three Rs

- Guess the meaning of the idiom in the dialogue below.

Ben: How can I raise my grades? Any tips for me?

Suzie: I think you should focus on the basic subjects, which are <u>the three *Rs*</u>, first.

Ben: What are they?

Suzie: Reading, writing, and arithmetic?

Ben: I see.

L.M(표면적 의미)	F.M(비유적 의미)
세 가지 R	the basic subjects taught at school; reading, writing, and arithmetic; 학교에서 제공되는 기초적 과목인 읽기, 쓰기, 산수(계산) 과목

- History: 영국의 시장이었던 William Curtis의 일화에서 유래함. 교육을 중시했던 그는 교육부처에서 마련된 공적 저녁 모임에서 교육에서 세 가지 R이 중요하다고 건배사를 했는데, Riting(writing), Reading, Rithmetic(arithmetic)을 뜻함. 사실은 그가 철자를 잘못 알았던 데에서 기인하지만, 그 자리에 있었던 기자는 그 시장을 매우 기민한 사람이라고 주장하였고, 사람들 또한 그가 일부러 잘못된 철자로 말한 것처럼 생각하여 Curtis는 많은 박수갈채를 받았다고 함.

♣ Make your own dialogue.

⊚ rack one's brains

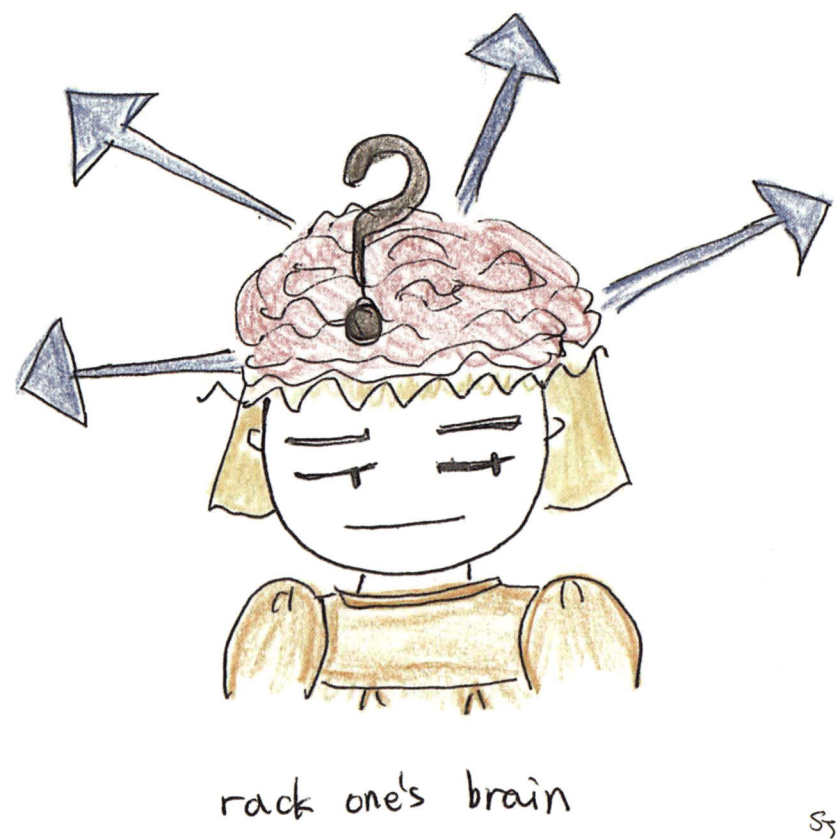

– Guess the meaning of the idiom in the dialogue below.
Ben: Suzie's birthday is coming. What should we get her?
William: Let's *rack our brains* to find a perfect gift for her.

L.M(표면적 의미)	F.M(비유적 의미)
머리를 뒤틀어지게 하다/ 괴롭히다	to stretch the brain beyond its normal limits, in order to remember something, to find something appropriate to say, etc; 적절한 말을 찾기 위해서 또는 기억해 내기 위해서 보통의 한계를 넘어서 머리를 쓰다/머리를 짜내서 생각하다

– History: 17세기 고문 기구로 사용되었던 rack은 롤러가 끝에 달려 있어서 사지를 묶고 점점 더 당겨서 신체를 늘려 괴롭게 만드는 기구였는데, 마치 신체의 한계를 늘리듯이 머리의 한계를 넘어 머리를 쓴다는 데에서 유래함.

♣ Make your own dialogue.

◉ to rain cats and dogs

- Guess the meaning of the idiom in the dialogue below.

Ben: It is <u>raining</u> cats and dogs.

Suzie: I guess the rainy season has just set in!

L.M(표면적 의미)	F.M(비유적 의미)
고양이와 개떼로 비가 내리다	to rain hard, extremely heavily; 비가 많이/심하게 내리다(폭우가 내리다)

- History: 지난 세기에는 하수 시설이 불량하여 폭풍우가 쏟아지면 길에 떠돌던 동물들(개나 고양이)의 무리들이 홍수와 함께 떠내려왔다는 이미지에서 유래함.

♣ Make your own dialogue.

◉ in the red

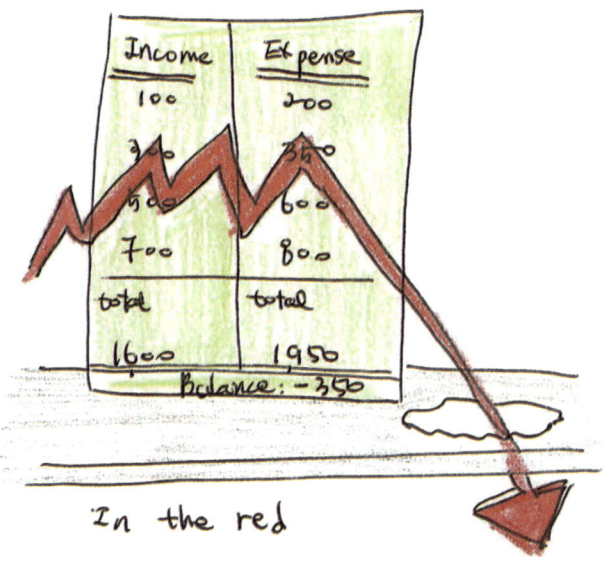

- Guess the meaning of the idiom in the dialogue below.

Ben: I'm already in the red this month.
Suzie: It's only the beginning of the month. What's wrong?
Ben: I think I've been spending too much.

L.M(표면적 의미)	F.M(비유적 의미)
빨강으로	in debt, overdrawn; 빚을 진, 초과 인출된

- History: 1920년대에 미국에서 쓰이기 시작한 표현으로, 회계 장부에 빚이나 적자를 표시할 때 전통적으로 사용했던 색상이 빨강인 데서 유래함. (in the black - 신용을 기록하는 색상으로는 검정이 사용되었다고 함. 흑자(이윤)라는 뜻임)

♣ Make your own dialogue.

◎ **to read between the lines**

- Guess the meaning of the idiom in the dialogue below.

Ben: I think William is upset with me. He gave me a letter, but I still don't know what I did wrong to him.

Suzie: Let me see…. You need to *read* between the lines.

Ben: Why didn't he just spell it out for me? If so, it could be easier to understand how he feels.

L.M(표면적 의미)	F.M(비유적 의미)
문장 사이(행간)를 읽다	to discover the intended or real meaning beyond the obvious; 분명한 뜻을 넘어선 의도적이거나 진짜 의미를 발견하다

- History: 암호 해독 술의 한 방법으로, 글 안에 문장을 번갈아 비밀 메시지를 숨겨 두고 전체로부터 추출해 냈던 데에서 유래함.

♣ Make your own dialogue.

⊙ a red herring

- Guess the meaning of the idiom in the dialogue below.

Ben: I talked on the phone with Mary for three hours last night.
Suzie: What for?
Ben: She asked for me some tips on how to ask William out.
Suzie: I thought she has a crush on you. Isn't it just *a red herring*?
Ben: No way!

L.M(표면적 의미)	F.M(비유적 의미)
붉은 청어	anything which diverts (usually intentionally) attention away from the main argument; 주요 논쟁으로부터 딴 곳으로 주의(이목)를 돌리기 위한 것(주로 의도적임)

- History: 19세기의 표현으로, 청어를 말리고 저염한 뒤 훈제하면 붉은 갈색 빛을 띠게 되는데, 이 청어는 강한 냄새를 가지게 되어 때때로 사냥개가 냄새를 따르는 훈련을 하는 데에 사용된 데에서 유래함.

♣ Make your own dialogue.

Idioms from A to Z: R

⊙ a red-letter day

a red-letter day

- Guess the meaning of the idiom in the dialogue below.

Suzie: Why is July 4th a red-letter day in America?

Ben: Oh, it's Independence Day. It's a day to celebrate America's independence from Britain.

Suzie: I see…. In Korea's case, Independence Day falls on August 15th.

L.M(표면적 의미)	F.M(비유적 의미)
빨강으로 표시된 날	a day-to-celebrate, a day of special significance; 축제일, 특별한/중요한 날

- History: 15세기 동안에 보통의 날은 검은색으로 표기하였지만, 모든 축제일이나 성인의 날을 달력에 빨간색으로 표시한 데에서 관습처럼 시행됨.

♣ Make your own dialogue.

◉ to **ring a bell**

― Guess the meaning of the idiom in the dialogue below.

Suzie: Do you remember Steve?

Ben: Steve who?

Suzie: The boy who was at Green High School.

Ben: Doesn't *ring a bell*. Can you tell me more about him?

L.M(표면적 의미)	F.M(비유적 의미)
종을 치다	to remind someone of something, to jog someone's memory; 어떤 것을 생각나다, 기억해 내다

― History: 사무실 등에서 종을 침으로써, 이목을 집중시켰던 데에서 유래하여, 기억 속 멀리 저장되었던 봤거나 말했던 것을 갑자기 기억해 내는 것으로 사용됨.

♣ Make your own dialogue.

⊙ to ride roughshod over

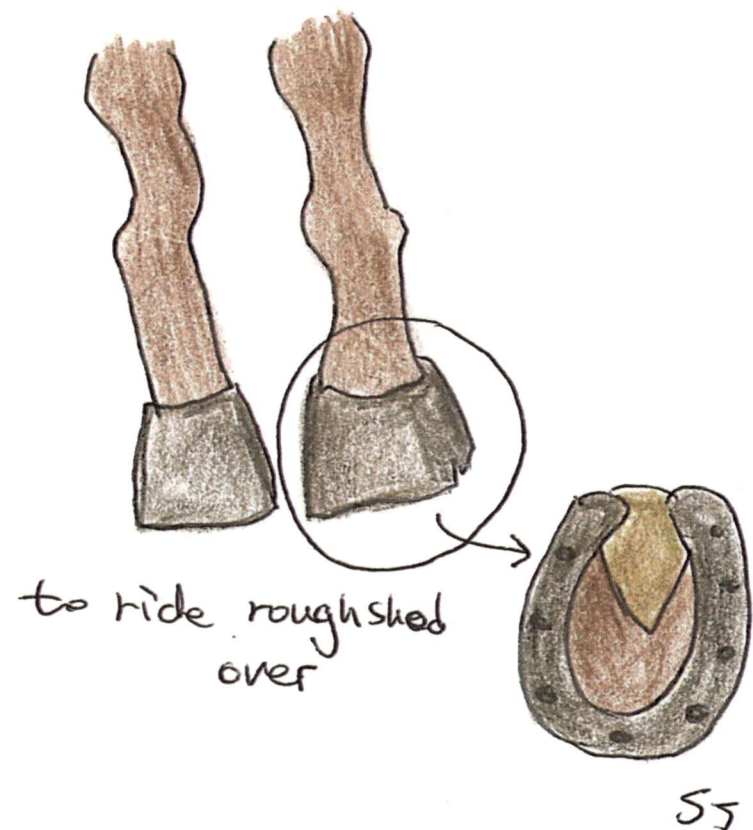

- Guess the meaning of the idiom in the dialogue below.

Suzie: William stood me up yesterday.

Ben: Again?

Suzie: I think he must be *riding roughshod* over me.

Ben: You should complain to him about it.

L.M(표면적 의미)	F.M(비유적 의미)
스파이크 있는 편자를 단 말을 타다	to behave in an arrogant and domineering manner towards someone; 다른 사람을 업신여기고 함부로 대하다

- History: 말의 편자에 못이 튀어나온 듯한 스파이크를 단 경우는 원래 미끄럽거나 언 땅에 미끄러짐을 방지하기 위해서 사용되었는데, 기마대의 말들의 경우는 적의 군사들이 말에서 떨어졌을 때, 적군을 말이 밟고 지나갈 때 심한 상처(부상)를 입히기 위한 목적으로도 사용되었다고 함.

♣ Make your own dialogue.

⊙ to ring true/false

- Guess the meaning of the idiom in the dialogue below.

Suzie: The gossip is that Tom Cruise bought a house in Seoul.
Ben: For real? It doesn't *ring true*, though. However, if it's true, I wish I could see him in person in Seoul once in my life time.

L.M(표면적 의미)	F.M(비유적 의미)
진실/거짓처럼 들리다	to give the appearance of being genuine and authentic, or not; 정말처럼 들리다, 진실처럼 또는 있을 것 같은 일처럼 들리다

- History: 옛날에는 동전을 주조했을 때, 순수한 금속 물질만을 사용했는데, 동전이 잘 만들어졌는지 확인할 때 딱딱한 바닥에 동전을 떨어뜨렸을 때 들리는 소리로 구분하였다는 데에서 유래함.

♣ Make your own dialogue.

⊚ to know/learn the ropes

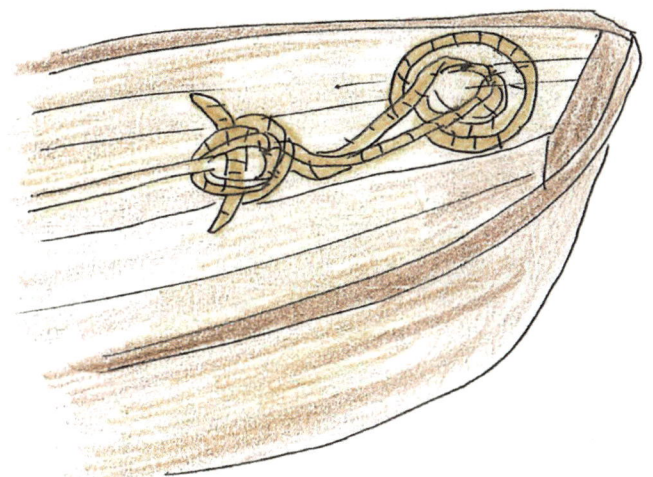

− Guess the meaning of the idiom in the dialogue below.

Suzie: Wow, you bought a new smart phone.

Ben: Yes. To get used to this new phone, I need to know the ropes first.

L.M(표면적 의미)	F.M(비유적 의미)
밧줄을 다루는 방법을 알다/배우다	to know/learn how to perform a task skillfully; 과제를 기술적으로(능숙하게) 수행하는 방법을 알다/배우다

− History: 항해 용어로써, 배의 닻줄 장치는 매우 복잡한 구조로, 선원들이 배를 운전하기 위해서는 밧줄 사용에 익숙해졌어야 한다는 데에서 유래함.

♣ Make your own dialogue.

◎ to sell someone down the river

– Guess the meaning of the idiom in the dialogue below.

Suzie: I was upset with Sam.

Ben: What for?

Suzie: He promised me that he would help me with my final project. However, I knew he was already working with Jane for the project.

Ben: I heard that Jane treated Sam for a fancy dinner.

Suzie: He <u>sold me down the *river*</u> for the dinner.

L.M(표면적 의미)	F.M(비유적 의미)
강가에서 사람을 매매하다	to betray someone, usually for one's own profit; 자신의 이익을 취하기 위해서 다른 사람을 배신하다

– History: 북미 지역의 남쪽 지방에서 유래한 표현으로, 1808년에 노예 제도가 폐지되었음에도, 여전히 목화나 설탕 농장에서 많은 노동을 필요로 했던 남부 지방에서는 암암리에 노예를 사용하였고 노예 매매가 이뤄졌는데, 북쪽 지방의 더 이상 필요치 않았던 노예들을 미시시피강 남부 지방으로 이동시켜 팔았던 데에서 유래함.

♣ Make your own dialogue.

Idioms from A to Z: R

⊙ between a rock and a hard place

− Guess the meaning of the idiom in the dialogue below.

Suzie: I'm <u>between a *rock* and a hard place.</u>

Ben: Why?

Suzie: I want to skip classes, but I have to go see the doctor to submit a document to prove that I am sick to school. At the hospital, the doctor will give me an injection. I really hate it.

Ben: So you mean…. You don't want to either go to school or go see a doctor.

Suzie: Yep. That's what I'm saying. What should I do?

L.M(표면적 의미)	F.M(비유적 의미)
바위와 딱딱한(굳은) 장소 사이에	in a delemma, between two unpalatable alternatives; 진퇴양난의, 딜레마의/Catch 22와 비슷하게 사용됨.

− History: 1921년에 출간되었던 미국 방언을 다룬 책에서 원래는 'to be bankrupt(파산한)'의 의미로 사용되었음. 20세기의 초반에 재정적인 불안의 시대에 애리조나주에서 처음 사용되었다고 하는데, 20세기 후반에 와서는 의미가 다르게 사용되기 시작함.

♣ **Make your own dialogue.**

⊙ to cry/ proclaim/shout something from the rooftops

- Guess the meaning of the idiom in the dialogue below.

Suzie: Yumi got pregnant.
Ben: Good for her! She was looking forward to it.
Suzie: Yes, but she wants to keep it as a secret for now until she enters a stable phase of pregnancy.
Ben: When she <u>cries it from the *rooftops*</u>, let's give her a big party to celebrate her.
Suzie: Of course!

L.M(표면적 의미)	F.M(비유적 의미)
지붕 위에서 소리 지르다	to make something known publicly; 사람들이 알게 하다, 어떤 것을 공개하다

- History: 성경의 누가복음에 예수님이 '위선을 통해 숨겨진 모든 것은 언젠가 다 알려지게 된다'라는 말을 한 데에서 유래함. 예수님의 말씀 중에 '집의 꼭대기에서 외쳐질 것이다'라는 말을 인용하여 이디엄으로 사용하게 되었는데, 비탈진 유럽의 지붕 구조와 달리 팔레스타인 지역에서는 지붕이 평평하여 지붕 위에서 소리 지르기가 더 수월했다고 함. 현재에는 'proclaim'이라는 단어 대신 흔히 많이 사용되는 'cry'나 'shout'가, 'housetops' 대신 'rooftops'가 대체되어 사용된다고 함.

♣ Make your own dialogue.

Idioms from A to Z: R

⊙ to cross the Rubicon

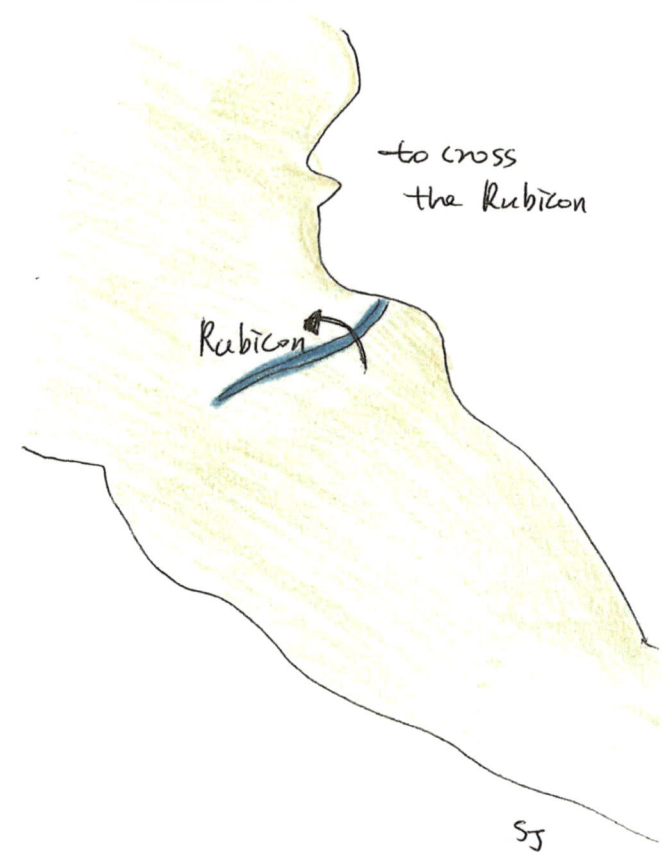

- Guess the meaning of the idiom in the dialogue below.

Suzie: Are you sure that you won't regret quitting your current job? You have worked there more than 10 years, so I think you reconsider it before you <u>cross the *Rubicon*</u>.

Ben: I already handed in a letter of resignation.

L.M(표면적 의미)	F.M(비유적 의미)
루비콘 강을 건너다	to take a step or decision from which there is no turning back; 퇴로가 없는 결정이나 행보를 취하다

- History: 고대 시대에 이탈리아와 시저의 영토의 경계에는 루비콘 강이 흘렀는데, 당시 군대들은 로마에 충성한다는 의미로 루비콘강을 건널 때는 반드시 무장을 해제하고 건넜는데, 무장했다는 의미는 즉, 전쟁을 선포한다는 뜻으로 받아들여졌다고 함. 집정관 연임을 거부당한 시저는 충성심이 강하고 확고한 의지를 지녔던 신하들에 힘입어 군사를 이끌고 루비콘 강을 건넜는데, 이는 전쟁을 선포한 의미와 같기 때문에 다시 되돌릴 수 없는 결과를 초래할 거라는 데에서 유래함.

♣ Make your own dialogue.

Idioms from A to Z: R

⊙ a/the **rule** of thumb

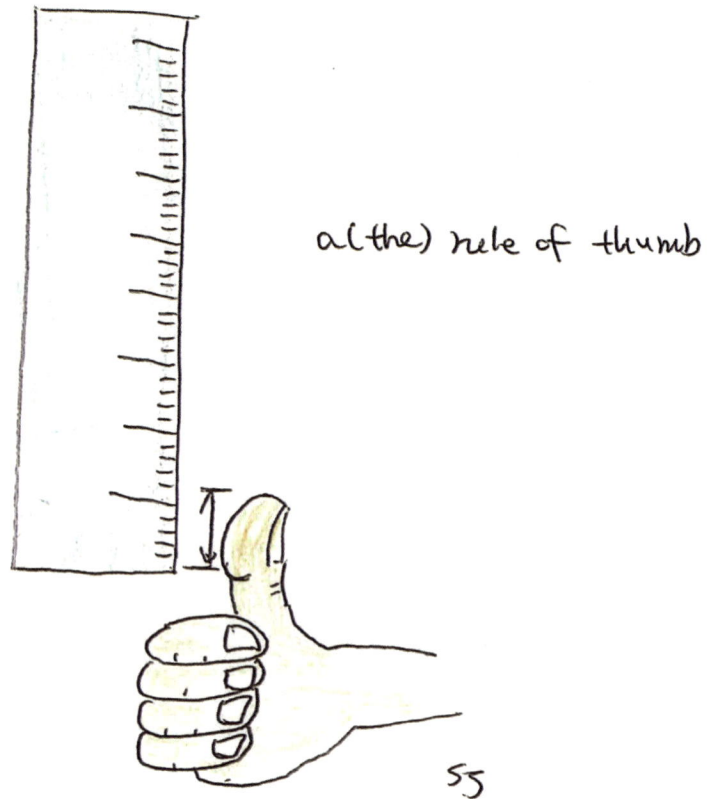

− Guess the meaning of the idiom in the dialogue below.

Suzie: I don't know what to choose among these T-shirts.

Ben: As a _rule_ of thumb, just choose the one that catches your eye at first sight.

Suzie: Thanks for your tip.

L.M(표면적 의미)	F.M(비유적 의미)
엄지손가락 자(rule)	guesswork, rough calculation, estimate based on experience rather than careful calculation; 대략의 계산, 추측, 주의 깊은 계산보다는 경험에 바탕으로 한 추산(정)

− History: 십진법의 도량법이 개발되기 전에 사람들이 치수를 측량할 때는 엄지손가락의 첫 번째 마디를 사용하였다는 데에서 유래함.

♣ **Make your own dialogue.**

Idioms from A to Z: R

Idioms from A to Z: S

-S-

♣ These are the List of Idioms S. Are there any idioms you already know? If not, try to guess the meaning of the idioms below.

- to get the **sack**/to give someone the **sack** ☐
- (in) **sackcloth** and ashes ☐
- **salad** days ☐
- to be worth one's **salt** ☐
- the **salt** of the earth ☐
- to take **something** with a pinch/grain of **salt** ☐
- the **seamy side** ☐
- to **scratch** the **surface** ☐
- (to **start**) from **scratch** ☐
- in a **shambles** ☐
- to **separate** the **sheep** from the goats ☐

- three **sheets** to the wind ---------------------------- ☐
- to keep one's **shirt** on ---------------------------- ☐
- (to live) on a **shoestring** ---------------------------- ☐
- to give/get a **short shrift** ---------------------------- ☐
- the **silly season** ---------------------------- ☐
- to be born with a **silver spoon** in one's mouth ------------ ☐
- to **sink** or **swim** ---------------------------- ☐
- a **sitting** duck ---------------------------- ☐
- a **skeleton** in the cupboard/closet ---------------------- ☐
- on **skid** row ---------------------------- ☐
- by the **skin** of one's teeth ---------------------------- ☐

- to have **something** up one's **sleeve** ---------------- ☐
- to laugh up one's **sleeve** ------------------------------ ☐
- **sour** grapes -- ☐
- to go for a **song** -- ☐
- to **sow** one's wild oats --------------------------------- ☐
- to throw a **spanner** in the works ------------------- ☐
- to put a **spoke** in **someone**'s wheel -------------- ☐
- to throw in the **sponge** --------------------------------- ☐
- hit the **spot** -- ☐
- a **storm** in a teacup ------------------------------------- ☐
- up the **spout** --- ☐

- ⊙ (go) back to **square** one ---------------------------------- ☐
- ⊙ a **stalking** horse -- ☐
- ⊙ **steal** a march (up(on)) ------------------------------------ ☐
- ⊙ made of **sterner stuff** ------------------------------------- ☐
- ⊙ to leave no **stone** unturned -------------------------------- ☐
- ⊙ to **strain** at a gnat and **swallow** a camel --------------- ☐
- ⊙ a **swan song** --- ☐
- ⊙ the **sword** of Damocles ------------------------------------- ☐

◉ to get the sack/to give someone the sack

to get the sack

- Guess the meaning of the idiom in the dialogue below.

Suzie: The Korean economy is getting worse and worse.

Ben: I know…. We still remain in office, but no one knows when we'll get the sack.

L.M(표면적 의미)	F.M(비유적 의미)
포대 자루를 받다/누군가에게 포대 자루를 주다	to be dismissed/to dismiss someone from their job; 해고된/누군가를 직장(일)에서 자르다

- History: 옛날 장인은 모든 자신의 도구를 포대 자루에 넣어서 그의 고용인이 있는 작업장에 두었는데, 장인의 실수든 작업 부족이든 간에 일에서 잘리면 고용주는 그 장인에게 장인의 도구를 담은 포대 자루를 다시 돌려줬다는 데에서 유래함.

♣ Make your own dialogue.

⊙ (in) sackcloth and ashes

(in) sackcloth and ashes　　　　SJ

- Guess the meaning of the idiom in the dialogue below.

Suzie: What do you expect from a newly elected president?

Ben: I just hope he could lead people in *sackcloth* and ashses. Many people have been suffering since the Covid-19 pandemic.

L.M(표면적 의미)	F.M(비유적 의미)
마대(베) 옷을 입고	(a visible expression of) petinence; 보이는 표현 방식으로의 참회/후회

- History: 성경을 통해 익숙해진 히브리 관습에서 암시된 것으로, 마대를 입는다는 것은 애도와 참회를 의미한다고 함. 마대는 곡물을 담던 자루로 사용되었던 거친 염소 털로 만들어졌는데, 그것을 입는 것은 겸손(비하)의 의미로 받아들여졌다고 한 데서 유래함.

♣ Make your own dialogue.

⊙ salad days

- Guess the meaning of the idiom in the dialogue below.

Suzie: Look at this photo! We look very young and vibrant.
Ben: Yeah, it has been 5 years since this photo was taken. Those were our <u>*salad days*</u>! Miss them so much!

L.M(표면적 의미)	F.M(비유적 의미)
샐러드의 날	one's days of youth and inexperience; 미숙한 어린(풋내기) 시절

- History: Green은 15세기 이래로 'youthful(젊음)'을 상징하는 말로 사용되었음. 셰익스피어가 '안토니오와 클레오파트라'라는 극본을 썼을 때, 클레오파트라의 대사 중 자신의 salad days를 언급한 말에서, "When I was green in judgement, cold in blood."라고 비유하였던 데에서 유래되었는데, 19세기 후반에 말이 유행하게 되었음. 영국의 엘리자베스 2세 여왕이 한 연설에서 이 말을 인용하여 다시 유명하게 됨.

♣ Make your own dialogue.

⊙ to be worth one's salt

- Guess the meaning of the idiom in the dialogue below.

Ben: I think I got a raise.
Suzie: Good for you! You are worth your *salt*.
Ben: Thanks.

L.M(표면적 의미)	F.M(비유적 의미)
소금만큼의 가치가 있는	capable, deserving of one's position or salary; 지위나 연봉을 받을 만큼 능력 있는

- History: 'salary'는 'salt'를 뜻하는 라틴어인 'salarium'에서 나온 말로, 'salt money'라는 돈이 로마 병정에게 지급되면 그들은 그 돈으로 소금을 구입하여 음식에 맛을 더하고 건강을 유지하였다는 데에서 유래함. 즉, 소금이 그만큼의 가치가 있다는 데에서 사람의 능력을 빗댄 것에서 유래함.

♣ Make your own dialogue.

⊙ the salt of the earth

− Guess the meaning of the idiom in the dialogue below.

Suzie: Congrats on your new baby!
Sunny: Thanks.
Suzie: How do you want your baby to grow old?
Sunny: I just hope that he will be the *salt* of the earth.
Suzie: He will.

L.M(표면적 의미)	F.M(비유적 의미)
세상(이 땅)의 소금	(of a person(s)) unpretentious yet praiseworthy, fundamentally good; 세상의 소금과 같은 세상에 도움을 주는 인격적으로 훌륭한 사람

− History: 성경 중 마태복음에서 예수님이 말씀하신 데에서 유래함. '너는 the salt of the earth(세상의 소금)와 같은 존재이다. 하지만 소금의 맛이 사라진다면, 어떤 것으로 소금 간을 할 수 있겠느냐? 그때부터는 땅에 뿌려지고 사람에 발에 밟히는 그런 아무 쓸모도 없는 존재가 되는 것이다.'

♣ Make your own dialogue.

⊙ to take something with a pinch/grain of salt

- Guess the meaning of the idiom in the dialogue below.

Ben: What do you think of what Sam just said?

Suzie: I usually <u>take it with a pinch of *salt*</u> whenever Sam says something.

L.M(표면적 의미)	F.M(비유적 의미)
무언가에 약간의 소금을 가져가다	to be sc(k)eptical about something, to entertain doubts; 어떤 것에 대해 의심하다/액면 그대로 받아들이지 않다/ 반신반의하다

- History: 폼페이가 쟁취한 왕궁에 왕의 책상 위에서 독약의 해독제를 찾은 데에서 유래하였는데, 그 재료 중에 약간의 소금이 포함되었다고 함. 실제 옛날부터 소금은 해독 작용을 하는 것으로 알려져 사용되었다고 함. 소금을 흩뿌리면 음식을 더 맛있게 만들듯이, 의심스러운 이야기나 핑계도 더 쉽게 넘어갈 수 있다고 여겨짐.

♣ Make your own dialogue.

◎ the seamy side

the seamy side   SJ

- Guess the meaning of the idiom in the dialogue below.

Ben: Yumi always looks happy on her SNSs.

Suzie: She may not be in her life. How can people be happy all the time in real life?

Ben: Yeah! We don't know <u>*the seamy side*</u> of their life on SNSs.

L.M(표면적 의미)	F.M(비유적 의미)
바느질한 부분	the lowest, most degraded side of life: 삶의 이면(어두운/괴로운)

- History: 셰익스피어의 *Othello*(오텔로)의 Emilia가 옷의 안감 쪽에 느슨하게 바느질한 부분이 바깥에 노출된 것에 대해서 남편과 이야기한 대사에서 인용된 문구에서 유래하였음.

♣ Make your own dialogue.

◉ to scratch the surface

− Guess the meaning of the idiom in the dialogue below.

Ben: How did the counseling with your teacher go? Was it about your grades on the last tests?

Suzie: I felt like she **scratched** the **surface** about that matter. I realized that everything depends on my determination.

L.M(표면적 의미)	F.M(비유적 의미)
표면(층)을 긁다	to deal with a matter very superficially; 어떠한 문제를 매우 피상적으로(깊지 않게) 다루다/대하다

− History: scratch는 표면 위에 난 얄팍한(깊지 않은) 상처(자국)을 뜻하는데, 17세기부터는 '매우 가볍게 땅의 고랑을 만들다'라는 행위를 함으로써 사실은 대부분의 농사에 적합하지 않은 피상적인(얕은) 농사 준비를 뜻하는 것으로 사용되었다고 함.

♣ Make your own dialogue.

Idioms from A to Z: S

⊙ (to start) from scratch

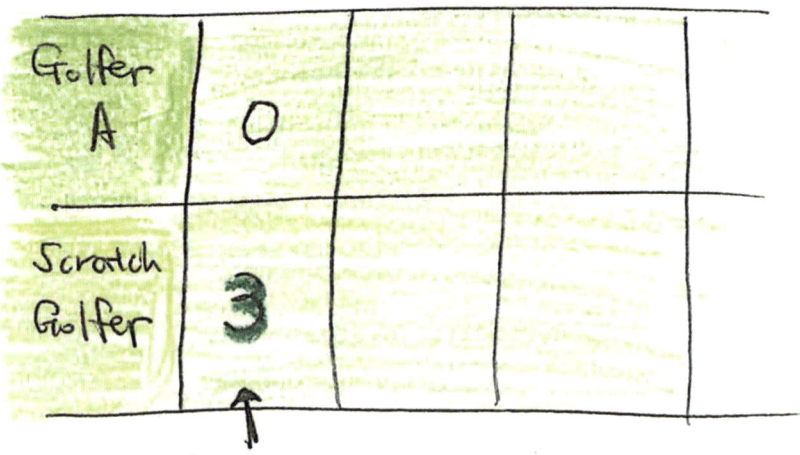

- Guess the meaning of the idiom in the dialogue below.

Ben: I visited Sam's bakery cafe, which opened recently.

Suzie: I did, too. I wonder how it was possible for Sam to open the cafe like that? It must cost a fortune to start a business. There must be some financial support from someone.

Ben: I don't know in detail, but as far as I know, he seems to _start_ his business from _scratch_.

L.M(표면적 의미)	F.M(비유적 의미)
시작 선에서 시작하다	to start from the very beginning with no help or advantage; 도움 없이 제로에서 시작하다 * scratch line: 육상 경주의 출발선(라인)

- History: 많은 스포츠 경기에서는 실력이 월등한 선수들에 비해 덜 숙련된 선수들을 위한 핸디캡 제도를 가지고 있는데, 19세기 후반에는 최고의 선수들의 시작 점수를 달리하는 방식을 테니스, 육상, 사이클 등의 여러 스포츠에서 사용하였음. 현재까지 골프 경기에서는 scratch golfer(핸디캡이 없는 실력 있는 선수)는 실력이 덜한 상대와 경기할 때 그들이 몇 차례 더 stroke(타격)할 수 있는 기회를 갖게 해 줌으로써 경기를 좀 더 매끄럽게(평등하게) 진행될 수 있도록 하고 있음.

♣ Make your own dialogue.

⊙ in a shambles

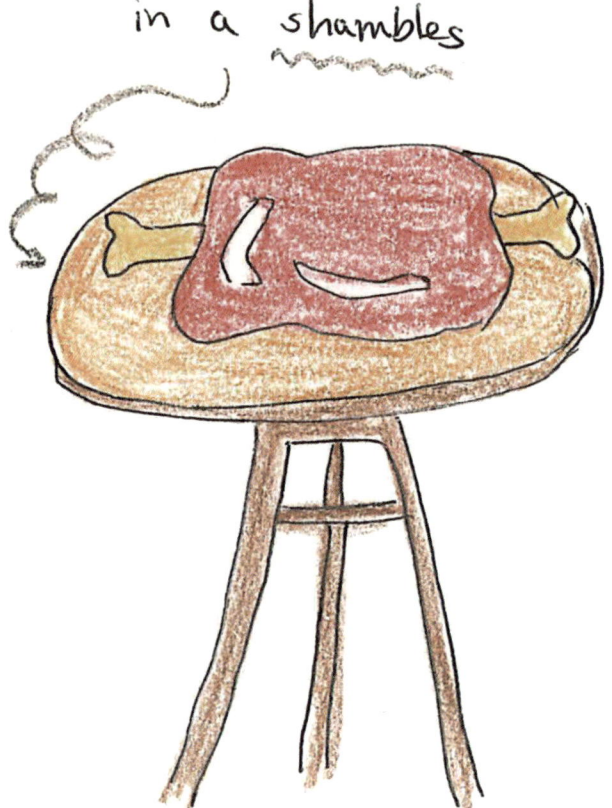

– Guess the meaning of the idiom in the dialogue below.

Suzie: I went to a department store on Black Friday.

Ben: Did you buy something good?

Suzie: Not much. All the items I wanted were almost sold out already. Actually, it was in a _shambles_ there, so it was almost impossible to shop there.

Ben: I can imagine….

L.M(표면적 의미)	F.M(비유적 의미)
지저분한 곳에서	in complete chaos, disarray; 완전한 혼돈, 무질서

– History: 상대방의 정책이나 업적을 비판하는 데 정치인들이 많이 애용하는 비유적인 표현임. 'shambles'는 정육점에서 고기를 보여 주기 위해서 올려두었던 'stool'을 뜻하였는데, 이런 정육점이 모여 있던 곳은 도축장처럼 살육과 유혈이 넘쳐나는 곳으로 묘사되었음. 현재에는 의미가 순화되어 '무질서', '혼란'의 의미로 바뀌어서 사용됨.

♣ Make your own dialogue.

Idioms from A to Z: S

⊙ to separate the sheep from the goats

- Guess the meaning of the idiom in the dialogue below.

Suzie: The results from the previous check-up aren't good.

Ben: You need to be more cautious about your health.

Suzie: What should I do first?

Ben: I think you eat unhealthy food. Why don't you start <u>*separating the sheep from the goats*</u> among the food you eat?

L.M(표면적 의미)	F.M(비유적 의미)
양들을 염소들로부터 떼어 두다 (구분하다)	to separate the good from the bad; 좋은 것과 나쁜 것을 구분(별)하다

- History: 양과 염소는 고기, 치즈, 털 등 다양한 쓰임으로 팔레스타인 지방에서는 둘 다 동등하게 가치를 인정받았었지만, 이 둘이 비유적으로 쓰일 때는 현격한 차이가 있었음. 마태복음에서 언급하듯이, 양은 보호와 안내를 필요로 하는 창조물인 데 반해 염소의 경우는 scapegoat(희생양)으로 쓰이는 것처럼 대표적인 죄나 비난 등을 나타낼 때 사용되었음. 따라서 양은 하나님에 속하는 것에 비하여 염소는 가치 없이 판단되는 것으로 여겼다는 데에서 유래함.

♣ Make your own dialogue.

Idioms from A to Z: S

⊙ three sheets to the wind

three sheets to the wind

— Guess the meaning of the idiom in the dialogue below.

Suzie: How are you today? I saw you drink a lot at the party last night.
Ben: People said that I was three *sheets* to the wind. A hangover is killing me.

L.M(표면적 의미)	F.M(비유적 의미)
바람을 따르는 세 개의 돛	very drunk; 매우 취한

-- History: 범선의 갑판 위에는, 돛의 방향을 조절하는 sheet이라고 불리는 밧줄이 있는데, 이 밧줄을 제대로 다루지 못하면 배를 조정할 수 없음. 항해할 때 바람을 더 만날수록 배는 더 불안정해지는데, 이 모습이 마치 술 취한 선원의 모습과 비슷하다고 한 데서 유래함. 술에 취한 정도를 sheet의 숫자로 표시하였음.

♣ Make your own dialogue.

⊙ to keep one's shirt on

— Guess the meaning of the idiom in the dialogue below.

Suzie: Parenting doesn't seem easy. How do you handle it?

Sunny: Everyday is like a war. I try to keep my shirt on when handling my kids.

L.M(표면적 의미)	F.M(비유적 의미)
셔츠를 입은 채로 있다	to keep calm; 평정심을 유지하다

— History: 싸움을 하고 싶어 안달 난 남자들은 셔츠가 더럽혀지고 찢어지는 것을 피하기 위해서 먼저 셔츠를 벗었다는 데에서 유래함.

♣ Make your own dialogue.

◉ (to live) on a **shoestring**

- Guess the meaning of the idiom in the dialogue below.

Suzie: I took a year off from my company.

Sunny: What for?

Suzie: I have overworked since I started to work there. I guess I burned myself out.

Sunny: You deserve a rest after all that hard work.

Suzie: Yeah. I like having a time for rest, but I don't like that I have to <u>live on a shoestring</u> during my leave of absence.

Sunny: You can't eat your cake and have it too.

L.M(표면적 의미)	F.M(비유적 의미)
신발 끈 정도만 겨우 살 정도로 돈을 아주 적게 쓰고 살다	to manage on very little money; to live on an unpredictable, low income; 아주 적은 돈을 관리하다; 예측할 수 없을 정도의 낮은 수입을 가지고 생활하다

- History: 자금이 너무 삭감되어서 길거리 노점상에서 싸게 살 수 있는 아이템 중 하나였던 신발 끈 정도만 겨우 살 정도의 돈만 가지고 있다는 데에서 유래함.

♣ Make your own dialogue.

◉ to give/get a short shrift

- Guess the meaning of the idiom in the dialogue below.

Suzie: When is the due date for our final project?

Ben: By 3 o'clock.

Suzie: What? We only have 30 minutes to go.

Ben: Right. We need to give a *short shrift* to finish it.

Suzie: Gotcha!

L.M(표면적 의미)	F.M(비유적 의미)
잠시의 여유를 주다/받다	to treat someone brusquely without hearing them out/to be dismissed out of hand; 가차 없이 다루다/서둘러 후다닥 처리하다

- History: 옛날에 범죄자들이 처형받기 전에 통상적으로 서둘러서 임종 고해(shrift)를 하였는데, 셰익스피어의 Richard III 연극에서 'shrift' 하는 장면이 언급된 데에서 유래함.

♣ Make your own dialogue.

⊙ the silly season

— Guess the meaning of the idiom in the dialogue below.

Suzie: What's the main news on the front page of the newspaper today?
Ben: Nothing special! There's a piece about newly-born quadruplets.
Suzie: The _silly season_ has just arrived.

L.M(표면적 의미)	F.M(비유적 의미)
어리석은(바보 같은) 계절 (시기)	the months of August and September when Parliament is not in session; 신문이 별 볼 일 없어지는 시기

— History: 보통 8~9월에 미국의 국회가 휴정하는 기간에는 정치적인 뉴스거리가 없어서, 그 기사를 대체하기 위해서 별로 중요하지 않은 뉴스로 채웠다는 데에서 유래함.

♣ Make your own dialogue.

⊙ to be born with a **silver spoon** in one's mouth

– Guess the meaning of the idiom in the dialogue below.

Suzie: Tom is a role model for the young and rich people.

Ben: He created a successful enterprise by himself.

Suzie: I thought he was rich because he <u>was born with a **silver spoon** in his mouth.</u>

L.M(표면적 의미)	F.M(비유적 의미)
은수저를 입에 물고 태어나다	to be born into a rich family; to be born lucky; 부자 가정에서 태어나다/행운아로 태어나다

– History: 교회에서 세례를 받는 아이에게 대부/모가 세례 선물로 스푼을 주었는데, 보통 스푼은 젖을 뗄 때 사용되었던 아이템이었음. 오직 부자들만이 은으로 된 스푼을 살 수 있었다고 함.

♣ Make your own dialogue.

Idioms from A to Z: S

⊙ to sink or swim

- Guess the meaning of the idiom in the dialogue below.

Suzie: I heard Jason went broke. Should we have helped him?

Ben: I think it is too late to help him. It's <u>sink</u> or <u>swim</u> for him.

L.M(표면적 의미)	F.M(비유적 의미)
가라앉거나 수영하기	to fail or survive; without external help: 외부의 도움 없이 실패하거나 생존하다, 죽기 아니면 살아남기

- History: 몇십 세기 전 마녀사냥에 사용되었던 방법에서 유래된 것으로, 마녀를 가리기 위해서 물에 던졌을 때, 물의 침례를 거부당하지 않아 물에 가라앉는 사람은 마녀가 아님이 밝혀지지만 결국 가라앉아 죽게 되고, 물에 떠서 살아남더라도 결국 물의 침례를 거부당한 자로써 마녀로 낙인찍혀 처형당한다는 것에서 유래함.

♣ Make your own dialogue.

◉ a sitting duck

- Guess the meaning of the idiom in the dialogue below.

William: I was pick-pocketed on the subway on the way to work.
Ben: Sorry to hear that. Were you wearing a backpack at that time?
William: Yes.
Ben: You shouldn't wear a backpack in a crowded place. You must have been a _sitting_ duck to a pickpocket.

L.M(표면적 의미)	F.M(비유적 의미)
앉아 있는 오리	an easy target; 쉬운 목표물, 봉

- History: 앉아 있는 오리는 사냥꾼에게 쉬운 사냥감으로 여겨졌듯이, 사람에 비유할 때는 언어 또는 신체적 공격에 취약한 대상을 나타낸다고 함. 20세기에 군대에서 많이 사용되었던 용어였고, 'a sitting target'이란 단어로도 많이 대체되어 사용됨.

♣ Make your own dialogue.

⊙ a **skeleton** in the cupboard/closet

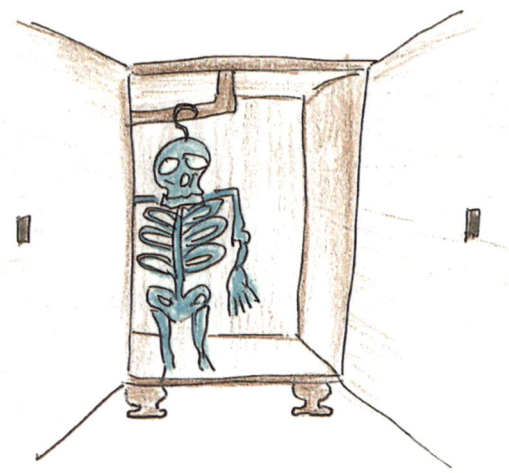

- Guess the meaning of the idiom in the dialogue below.

Suzie: I heard Sam dropped out of a high school.
Ben: Really?
Suzie: I think it is a _skeleton_ in the _cupboard_ about Sam.

L.M(표면적 의미)	F.M(비유적 의미)
옷장 속의 해골	a painful or shameful secret; 남의 이목을 꺼리는 집안의 수치, 어마어마한 비밀

- History: 19세기에 살인 피해자가 처참하게 찬장 속에 숨겨졌던 생생한 비유에서 유래함. 몇 년이 지나도 다시 찬장을 열게 되었을 때 뼈는 잔혹한 살인의 증거로 여전히 남게 되었다는 데에서 유래함.

♣ Make your own dialogue.

⊙ on skid row

- Guess the meaning of the idiom in the dialogue below.

Sam: The stock market crashed.
Ben: I know. In fact, I invested in stocks a lot.
Sam: Me, too. We are on *skid* row.

L.M(표면적 의미)	F.M(비유적 의미)
거친 목재가 지나간 자국	homeless, down-and-out; 빈털터리의, 노숙자의

- History: 공장으로 거친 목재를 운반해 갈 때 길에 남는 자국을 말하는데, 이런 벌목꾼들이 사는 동네는 보통 사창가나 낡은 술집이나 호텔이 즐비한 빈민굴이었다는 데에서 유래함. 'road' 대신에 'row'로 사용되기 시작함.

♣ **Make your own dialogue.**

⊙ by the skin of one's teeth

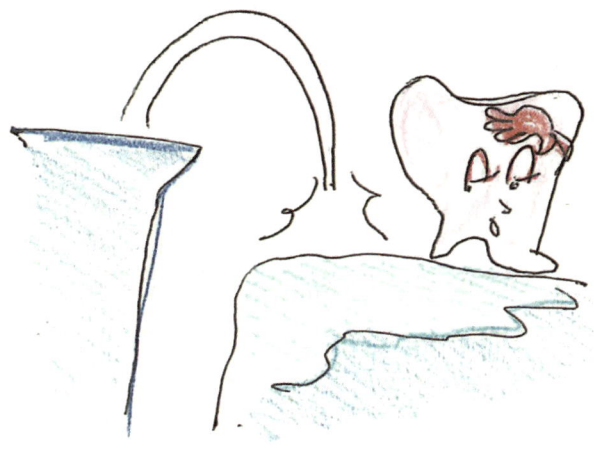

by the skin of one's teeth

– Guess the meaning of the idiom in the dialogue below.

Sam: How did the game go?

Ben: Our team won, but <u>by the *skin* of their teeth.</u>

L.M(표면적 의미)	F.M(비유적 의미)
치아의 표피만큼	just about, by the narrowest of margins; 위기일발의, 아슬아슬한(승리), 대접전

– History: 성경의 욥기(Job)에서 인용되었지만, 사실은 잘못 인용되어 사용되는 이디엄. Job이 의미한 것은 자신이 탈출하였을 때 아무것도 가져오지 못했다, 즉 '그의 가족, 친구, 소유물, 건강 등을 가져올 수 없었다'라고 의미한 것이었으나, 이 표현은 '매우 아슬아슬하게 탈출했다'는 의미로 잘못 해석되어 사용되고 있음.

♣ Make your own dialogue.

⊙ to have something up one's sleeve

- Guess the meaning of the idiom in the dialogue below.

Suzie: I didn't make a reservation for a flight and accommodation for our vacation yet.

Ben: What can we do? Do you *have **something** up your **sleeve**?*

L.M(표면적 의미)	F.M(비유적 의미)
누군가의 옷소매에 뭔가를 갖고 있다	to keep a resource concealed but in reserve; 나중에 필요할 때 쓰려고 계획/생각을 비밀로 하다, 유사시의 비법/해결책이 있다.

- History: 관객들을 놀라게 해 주기 위해서 소매 안에 모든 놀라움 거리를 숨겼던 마법사에게서 유래함.

♣ Make your own dialogue.

⊙ to laugh up one's *sleeve*

- Guess the meaning of the idiom in the dialogue below.

Suzie: Is there something wrong with me? Why are laughing up my *sleeve?*
Ben: My bad! Not at all! I just laughed because I just thought of a funny joke.

L.M(표면적 의미)	F.M(비유적 의미)
누군가의 옷소매를 보고 웃다	to laugh to oneself, to enjoy a private joke; 혼자 웃다(남몰래 웃다), 개인적인 농담을 즐기다/회심의 미소를 짓다

- History: 16세기 초반부터 사용되었던 표현으로, 당시에는 의상의 소매가 너무 넓어서, 조소를 하거나 낄낄거릴 비밀스러운 개인적인 웃음(미소)을 숨기기에 충분했다는 데에서 유래함.

♣ Make your own dialogue.

◉ sour grapes

- Guess the meaning of the idiom in the dialogue below.

Suzie: Did Sam make the audition?

Ben: I heard that he didn't attend it, saying that he didn't want it anymore.

Suzie: What? As far as I know, he really longed for it.

Ben: I think he is just a *sour grape*.

L.M(표면적 의미)	F.M(비유적 의미)
신 포도	comfort sought in despising what one would like for oneself but cannot have; 신 포도, 지기 싫어하는 마음(오기)

- History: 이솝 우화에서 높은 데 매달린 포도를 먹을 수 없어서 불쾌감을 느꼈던 여우가 "저 포도는 실 거야"라고 말했던 데에서 유래함.

♣ Make your own dialogue.

◎ **to go for a <mark>song</mark>**

– Guess the meaning of the idiom in the dialogue below.
Suzie: I sold my used jacket to a secondhand shop.
Ben: Did you make a good deal?
Suzie: I think it <u>went for a *song*</u> more than I expected.
Ben: That's bad.

L.M(표면적 의미)	F.M(비유적 의미)
노래의 값어치가 있다	to be sold very cheaply; below the true value; 실제 가치보다 낮게 매우 값싸게 팔리다

– History: 엘리자베스 1세 시대에는 오래된 발라드의 가치(격)가 동전 몇 개 정도로 아주 값싸게 여겨졌다고 함. Edmund Spenser가 *The Faerie Queen*이라는 작품에서 엘리자베스 여왕을 기리는 작품을 헌정하였는데, 여왕은 그의 재무상인 Cecil에게 그 작품에 대해서 500파운드를 지불하라고 명했음. Cecil은 그의 시에 대해서 그의 여류 명인(정부)보다 적은 돈을 가져갔는데, Spenser가 "고작 이게 노래(song)에 대한 전부냐?"라는 말을 한 것을 들었다는 데에서 유래함.

♣ Make your own dialogue.

⊙ to sow one's wild oats

to sow one's wild oats

— Guess the meaning of the idiom in the dialogue below.

Suzie: Didn't you know that Katie **_sowed_** her wild oats?
Ben: No way! She is the most successful businesswoman I've ever known.
Suzie: That's what I mean! People can change.

L.M(표면적 의미)	F.M(비유적 의미)
야생 귀리를 심다(뿌리다)	to spend one's youth in dissipation; 젊은 시절을 방탕하게 보내다

— History: 젊은 시절의 멍청한 행동은 결과를 초래하듯이, 잡초처럼, 야생 귀리는 한번 번식하면 제거하기 힘들다는 데에서 유래함.

♣ Make your own dialogue.

◉ to throw a spanner in the works

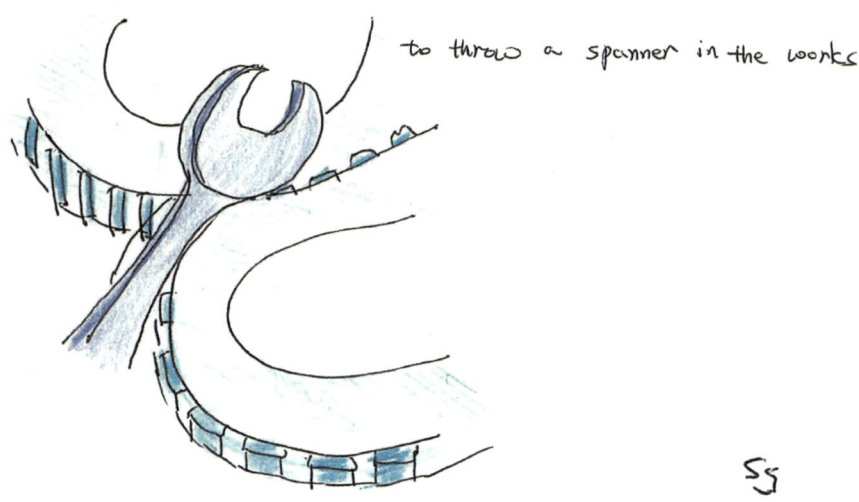

- Guess the meaning of the idiom in the dialogue below.

Suzie: I can't stand Sam anymore.

Ben: Why?

Suzie: He keeps throwing a spanner in the works for our school project.

L.M(표면적 의미)	F.M(비유적 의미)
기계 안에 스패너를 던져 넣는다	to upset the smooth running of something, to disrupt a plan or activity; 계획을 망치다/진행을 방해하다

- History: 산업 혁명 시대에 열악한 근무 조건을 견뎌온 저임금 공장 노동자들이 주로 사용했던 전략으로, 공장의 기계에 스패너(볼트와 너트를 죄는 도구)를 집어던져 기계를 고장 내거나 멈추게 했던 데에서 유래함.

♣ Make your own dialogue.

⊙ to put a spoke in someone's wheel

to put a spoke in someone's wheel

- Guess the meaning of the idiom in the dialogue below.

Suzie: William spilled the beans about Katie's birthday party.
Ben: Wasn't it supposed to be a secret among us?
Suzie: That's what I am saying. I doubted that he might put a *spoke* in our wheel.

L.M(표면적 의미)	F.M(비유적 의미)
누군가의 바퀴 안에 바큇살을 박아 넣는다	purposely to hinder someone's plans or success; 누군가의 계획이나 성공을 의도적으로 방해하다

- History: spoke(바큇살)은 바퀴의 필수 부품이기 때문에 왜 바큇살을 삽입하는 것이 진행을 방해하는지가 불확실하지만, 바큇살이 방향 회전을 방지하는 카트의 바퀴를 꿰찌르는 일종의 말뚝과 같은 역할을 한다는 데에서 유래함.

♣ Make your own dialogue.

⊙ to throw in the sponge

- Guess the meaning of the idiom in the dialogue below.

Suzie: I am having so much difficulty studying math for the upcoming exam.

Ben: Don't give up yet. It's too early to throw in the *sponge*. I will help you out.

Suzie: Thanks.

L.M(표면적 의미)	F.M(비유적 의미)
스펀지를 던져 넣는다	to give in, to admit defeat; 항복하다, 패배를 인정하다

- History: 19세기 중반에 권투 시합에서 유래한 말로, 복서가 많은 벌점을 받거나 패배를 인정할 준비가 되었을 때 자기편 선수를 지지하는 사람이 스펀지를 링에 던졌다는 데에서 유래하였는데, 현재는 수건(towel)을 던지는 것이 더 일상적으로 쓰이고 있음.

♣ Make your own dialogue.

Idioms from A to Z: S

⊙ hit the spot

- Guess the meaning of the idiom in the dialogue below.

Suzie: This pasta is so yummy.
Ben: Thanks. I cooked it from my mom's recipe.
Suzie: The taste hits the spot. Can I have more?

L.M(표면적 의미)	F.M(비유적 의미)
원하는 장소를 적중하다	to be just what was needed (usually referring to food or drink); 자신이 원하는 딱 그것이다, 바로 그대로다!

- History: 음식이나 음료의 만족감을 표현하기 위해서 만들어진 표현으로, spot은 특별히 원하던 맛을 기억하는 두뇌의 특별한 장소를 의미한다고 함.

♣ Make your own dialogue.

⊙ a storm in a teacup

- Guess the meaning of the idiom in the dialogue below.

Suzie: What was all the fuss about in the store?
Ben: Nothing serious. Tom didn't like the service.
Suzie: He is kinda sensitive about others' attitude toward him.
Ben: Also, he seems to like to raise *a storm in a teacup* for little things.

L.M(표면적 의미)	F.M(비유적 의미)
컵 잔 속의 폭풍	a petty disagreement, much fuss made about something of little importance; 괜한 소동

- History: 키케로에 의해서 "그는 포도주 국자로 휘저었다"라고 처음 표현되었던 것이, 17세기 이후로 여러 저명한 사람들에 의해서 여기저기 다양하게 즐겨 사용되었음.

♣ Make your own dialogue.

⊙ up the spout

- Guess the meaning of the idiom in the dialogue below.

Suzie: Sorry, Ben. I can't be with you for this vacation during the holidays.

Ben: How come?

Suzie: A schedule for the school orchestra recital has been advanced, so I have to attend practice during the holidays.

Ben: Well, that's my holiday plans gone up the *spout*!

L.M(표면적 의미)	F.M(비유적 의미)
리프트 위로다	in trouble, ruined, out of actions; 엉망이 되다, 일을 망치다

- History: 'spout'는 전당포에서 사용되는 리프트의 일종으로 맡겨지는 물건들은 그 리프트에 놓이고, 전당포 위에 있는 장소에 보관되었는데, 맡겨진 물건들은 원래 물건의 소유주가 돈을 갚기 전까지는 무용지물이라는 데에서 유래함.

♣ Make your own dialogue.

```
```

Idioms from A to Z: S

⊙ (go) back to **square** one

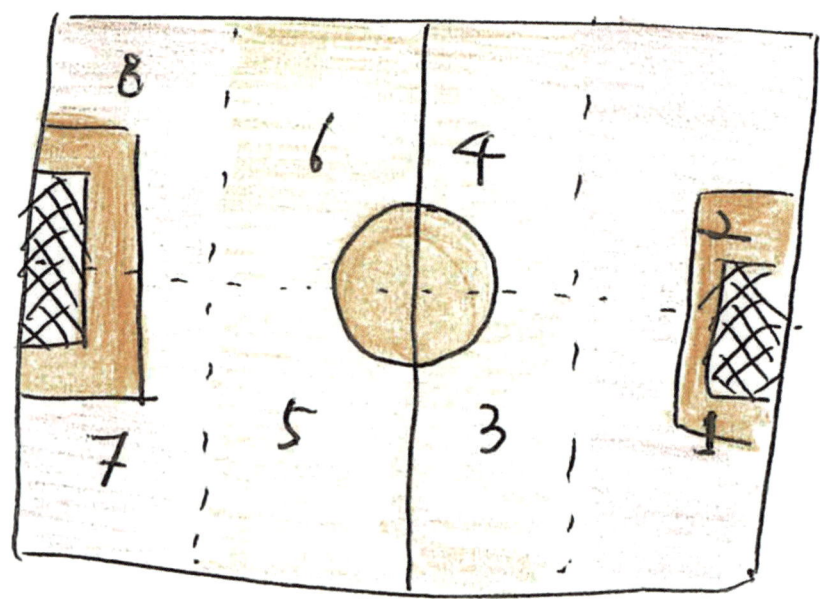

- Guess the meaning of the idiom in the dialogue below.

Suzie: The experiment we conducted failed.

Ben: Then, we should go back to *square* one. What was wrong?

L.M(표면적 의미)	F.M(비유적 의미)
1구역(원점)으로 돌아가다	to be back where one started with a project or plan; 계획이 처음으로 돌아가다, 원점으로 돌아가다

- History: TV가 발명되기 전, 라디오 축구 중계가 한창이었을 1920년대에는 말로만 중계를 하는 한계가 있어, 축구 경기장을 square로 구역을 나누어 각 번호를 붙여서 경기가 어디 구역에서 진행되는지를 알려주었다고 함. 'square 1'은 '최대한 이점을 잃는 구역'이었다고 하여, 'square 1' 구역에서는 점수를 원점으로 돌아간다는 의미로 상용되었다고 함. 하지만 1940년대에 와서 축구장의 grid(격자기준선)의 사용이 폐지되면서 점점 그 유래는 희미해져 갔음. 다른 유래로는, 'Snakes and Ladders'라는 게임으로, 어떤 square칸에 도달했을 경우 점수를 원점으로 돌린다고 한데서 유래하였다고 함.

♣ Make your own dialogue.

⊙ a stalking horse

- Guess the meaning of the idiom in the dialogue below.

Suzie: William was chosen as the class leader.

Ben: Does he have leadership?

Suzie: Why are you asking that?

Ben: I heard he is just a _**stalking** horse_ of Sam, so I kinda have doubts about his leadership.

L.M(표면적 의미)	F.M(비유적 의미)
남을 따라다니는 말	a person or pretext(핑계) designed as a cover for an ulterior action or motive or person, a mask for the true purpose; 구실, 위장, 허수아비 입후보자

- History: 중세 시대에는 사냥감에 몰래 접근하기 위해서 말 모양으로 만들어진 움직이는 스크린 뒤에서 사냥감에 몰래 접근하도록 말들이 훈련받았던 데에서 유래함.

♣ Make your own dialogue.

⊙ steal a march (up(on))

– Guess the meaning of the idiom in the dialogue below.

Suzie: Can I borrow *Holes*?

Ben: Oh, William already borrowed it.

Suzie: He ***stole a march*** again.

Ben: I will let you know when I get it back from William.

L.M(표면적 의미)	F.M(비유적 의미)
행진을 훔치다	to gain a furtive advantage; 숨겨진 이득을 취하다, 앞질러 행동하다, 선수를 치다

– History: Tudor 왕조(잉글랜드와 아일랜드 왕국을 다스린 군주를 5명 배출한 집안) 시대에는 행진을 하는 데 군대가 움직이는 거리는 하루 정도 걸렸었다고 함. 'gain a march upon the enemy'라고 하면 적군보다 하루 정도 먼저 행진한다는 의미이고, 'steal a march'는 적군이 기대치 못한 늦은 밤이나 이른 출발로 행진에 나선다는 데에서 유래했다고 함.

♣ Make your own dialogue.

◉ made of sterner stuff

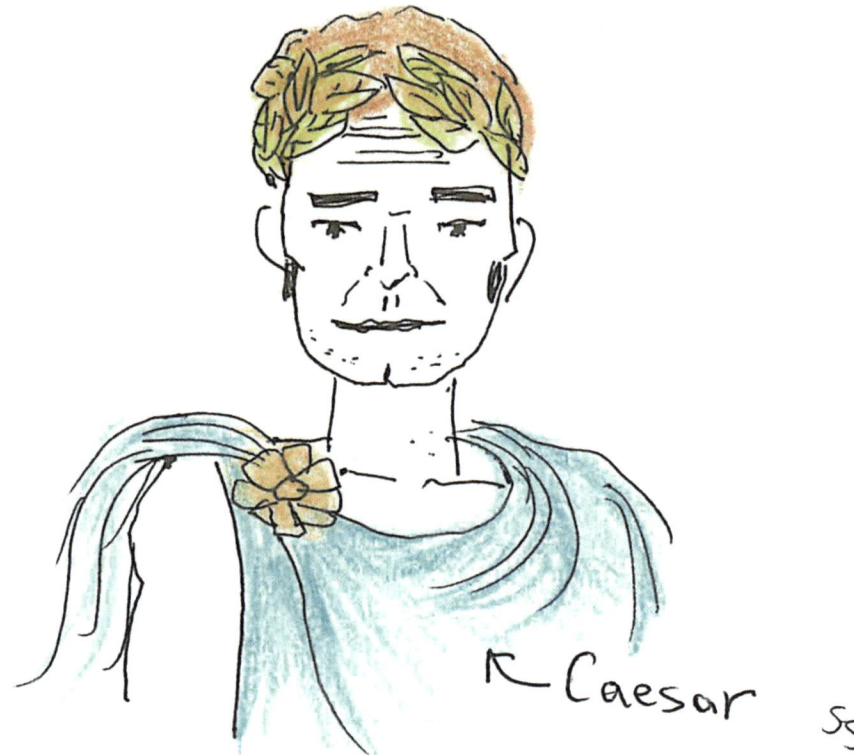

- Guess the meaning of the idiom in the dialogue below.

Suzie: How was the test?

Ben: I think I bombed it.

Suzie: Sorry to hear that. Try harder next time.

Ben: I will, but I'm worried about myself because I am not <u>made of **sterner stuff**</u> as you know.

Suzie: I hope you can stick to it this time.

L.M(표면적 의미)	F.M(비유적 의미)
강인한 물건(것)으로 만들어진	having a firm resolve, inflexible, unyielding; 확고 부동한, 불굴의 의지가 있는

- History: 셰익스피어의 줄리어스 시저 작품에서 사용된 표현. 시저가 성공적인 전투를 마치고 로마로 돌아오는데, 시저가 야망이 있어 스스로를 왕으로 추대할지 모른다고 두려움을 느꼈던 사람들 중에 공화당의 몇몇은 그가 왕이 되는 것을 막기 위해서 원로원에서 그를 죽일 음모를 꾸미고 실행에 옮겼음. 나중에 그런 그들의 계략을 알게 되어 화가 난 시저의 친구, 안토니우스는 시저의 장례식장에서 그들을 비꼬는 말을 정교하게 한 데에서 유래함. "시저는 야망이 있어 보였나요? 가난한 이들이 눈물을 흘렸을 때, 그는 같이 울어 주었습니다. 야망이란 더 강인한 것으로 만들어져야 하는 겁니다.(Did this in Caesar seem ambitious? When that the poor have cried, Caesar has wept; Ambition should be <u>made of **sterner stuff**.</u>)"

♣ Make your own dialogue.

Idioms from A to Z: S

◉ to leave no stone unturned

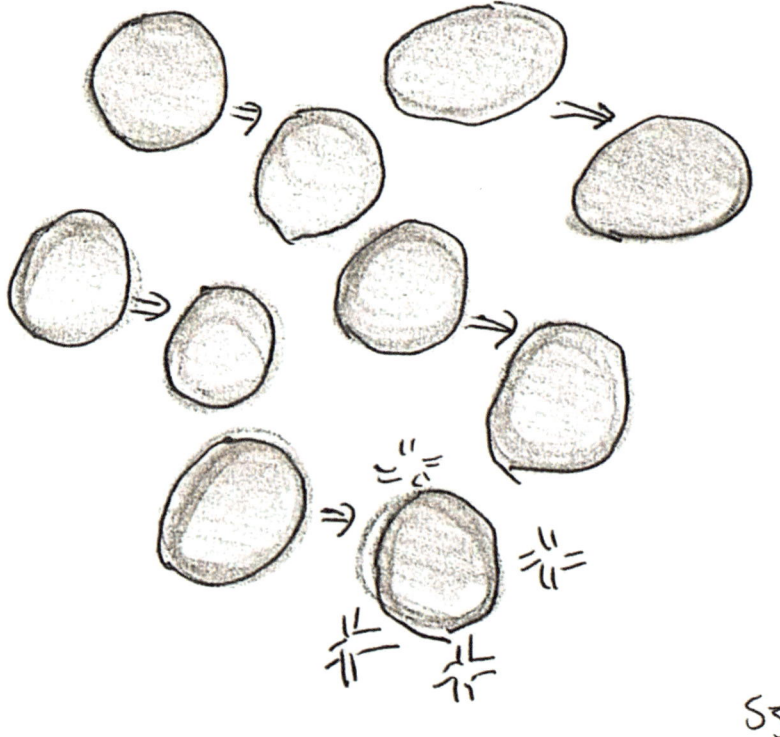

- Guess the meaning of the idiom in the dialogue below.

Suzie: Did you see my cellphone?

Ben: No.

Suzie: I left no *stone* unturned but I still couldn't find it.

Ben: Where was the place that you visited last?

L.M(표면적 의미)	F.M(비유적 의미)
안 뒤집어 놓은 돌들이 없도록 남기다	to make every effort possible to accomplish an aim; 목표를 성취하기 위해서 모든 노력을 기울이다, 구석구석 뒤지다

- History: 그리스 왕인 폴리크라테스는 페르시아와의 대승을 거두고, 페르시안 군의 막사에 남겨진 재물(보물)을 뒤지기 시작했는데 결국 찾지 못함. 델피의 신탁에게 어떻게 해야 할지 물어보았는데, 모든 돌을 다 뒤집어 보라고 하여 그는 다시 찾기 시작했고 결국 보물(재물)을 찾았다는 데에서 유래함.

♣ Make your own dialogue.

⊙ to strain at a gnat and swallow a camel

– Guess the meaning of the idiom in the dialogue below.

Suzie: How are your preparations going for a trip to the U.S.A?
Ben: I can't decide what to wear there.
Suzie: Did you book flights and hotels?
Ben: Speaking of which, I need to check if my reservations were confirmed.
Suzie: Oh! Ben, you seem to **_strain_** at a gnat and **_swallow_** a camel. When you prepare for something, try to weigh a matter and finish more important things first.

L.M(표면적 의미)	F.M(비유적 의미)
각다귀(하루살이)를 걸러내고 낙타를 삼키다	to be preoccupied with the trivial rather than the important, with details rather than major matters; 작은 일에 구애되어 큰일을 소홀히 하다

– History: 성경 Matthew에서 인용된 말로, 예수님은 법의 덜 중요한 부분에 대해서는 신경을 쓰면서도 정작 더 중요한 정의, 자비, 충의 등에 대해서는 신경을 쓰지 않는 점을 꼬집으며 말한 데에서 유래함.

♣ Make your own dialogue.

◉ a swan song

– Guess the meaning of the idiom in the dialogue below.

Suzie: How was the musical last night?

Ben: Everything was fantastic and at the curtain call, all the audience gave the main actor a standing ovation because it was his a ***swan song***.

Suzie: I should have been there.

Ben: It's too sad that we can't see him on the stage any more.

L.M(표면적 의미)	F.M(비유적 의미)
백조의 노래	a farewell appearance, performance, statement or work; 마지막 무대(작품)

– History: 고대인들은 백조는 울지 않지만, 죽음에 다다랐을 때 그들이 섬겼던 시와 노래의 신인 아폴로 신에게 다가갈 수 있다는 사실에 순수의 기쁨의 노래를 불렀다고 믿었던 데에서 유래함.

♣ Make your own dialogue.

⊙ the sword of Damocles

- Guess the meaning of the idiom in the dialogue below.

Suzie: I had a nightmare last night. I interpreted a dream, but it was not good at all.

Ben: You should be careful about <u>the *sword* of Damocles</u> today.

L.M(표면적 의미)	F.M(비유적 의미)
디모클레스의 칼	impending doom, an imminent threat; 다가올 운명, 신변에 가까운 위험(협)

- History: 시라쿠사의 왕이었던 디오니시오스의 총애를 얻기 위해서 극찬을 아끼지 않았던 다모클레스가 있었는데, 디오니시오스는 연찬에 그를 초대하여 그의 머리카락을 큰 칼에 매달아 묶고 앉게 하였음. 큰 칼이 위에 있어서 불안했던 다모클레스는 칼 때문에 불안해서 연찬을 즐길 수 없다고 이야기하자, 디오니시오스는 왕이라는 자리가 그런 언제 닥칠지 모르는 위협 속에서 살아가야 하는 자리라고 이야기했다는 전설에서 유래함.

♣ Make your own dialogue.

Idioms from A to Z: T

-T-

♣ These are the List of Idioms T. Are there any idioms you already know? If not, try to guess the meaning of the idioms below.

- at the end of one's **tether**/rope ---------------------- ☐
- not one's cup of **tea** ---------------------- ☐
- **through thick** and **thin** ---------------------- ☐
- to put on one's **thinking** cap ---------------------- ☐
- the **thin** end of the wedge ---------------------- ☐
- a **thorn** in the flesh/side ---------------------- ☐
- to hang by a **thread** ---------------------- ☐
- to give someone the **thumbs** up/down ---------------------- ☐
- to steal someone's **thunder** ---------------------- ☐
- to **tie** the knot ---------------------- ☐

- to **tilt** at windmills ----------------------------------- ☐
- in the nick of **time** ----------------------------------- ☐
- to **toe** the line ----------------------------------- ☐
- **tit** for **tat** ----------------------------------- ☐
- to grow like **Topsy** ----------------------------------- ☐
- **touch** wood ----------------------------------- ☐
- to come up/ **turn** up **trumps** ----------------------------------- ☐
- to **talk turkey** ----------------------------------- ☐

⊙ at the end of one's <u>tether/rope</u>

at the end of one's tether (rope)

— Guess the meaning of the idiom in the dialogue below.

Suzie: As the summer vacation approaches, students are getting out of control.

Ben: I feel that way, too. Teachers must be <u>at the end of their **tethers**(ropes).</u>

L.M(표면적 의미)	F.M(비유적 의미)
줄의 끝에	at the point of frustration, at the end of one's inner resources or powers of endurance; 인내심이 한계에 다다르다

— History: 'tether'는 떠돌아다니는 방목하는 동물(가축)의 자유를 제한하기 위한 줄을 가리킨 데서 유래함.

♣ Make your own dialogue.

◉ not one's cup of tea

- Guess the meaning of the idiom in the dialogue below.

Suzie: Neon items are in trend this season.

Ben: Neon color is <u>not my cup of *tea*</u>.

L.M(표면적 의미)	F.M(비유적 의미)
누군가의 찻잔이 아닌	취향이 아니다/좋아하지 않는다

- History: 차의 문화가 발달한 영국에서 유래한 말로 20세기에는 'my cup of tea'라는 표현은 '활기찬, 좋은 친구'를 의미하는 것으로 사용되었고 사람뿐만 아니라 '친밀함을 느끼는 물건'을 가리키는 의미로도 사용되었다고 함. 원래는 긍정적인 의미로 사용되었으나 2차 세계 대전 이후로 'not'과 결합하면서 'not my cup of tea'라는 표현이 쓰이면서 부정적인 의미로 쓰이게 되었다고 함.

♣ Make your own dialogue.

Idioms from A to Z: T

◉ through thick and thin

- Guess the meaning of the idiom in the dialogue below.

Suzie: Who is your ideal type? I mean your Miss Right?
Ben: A girl who is very kind to me **through thick** and **thin**.

L.M(표면적 의미)	F.M(비유적 의미)
두껍고 가는 것을 통하여	no matter what the difficulties, through good times and bad; 좋을 때나 궂을 때나, 시종일관

- History: 14세기에 쓰이기 시작한 말로, 여행자나 말이 빽빽한 잡목숲부터 덜 울창한 삼림 지대를 지나갈 때의 여러 종류의 땅을 묘사한 데에서 유래함.

♣ Make your own dialogue.

⊙ to put on one's **thinking** cap

- Guess the meaning of the idiom in the dialogue below.

Suzie: Did you decide where to go for your vacation?

Ben: Not yet. I need to put on my *thinking* cap.

L.M(표면적 의미)	F.M(비유적 의미)
생각하는 모자를 쓰다	to take time to consider, to mull things over; 심사숙고하다

- History: 17~19세기에 숙고해야 할 일이 있을 때 비유적으로 생각하는 모자를 썼던 데에서 유래함.

♣ Make your own dialogue.

◉ **the thin end of the wedge**

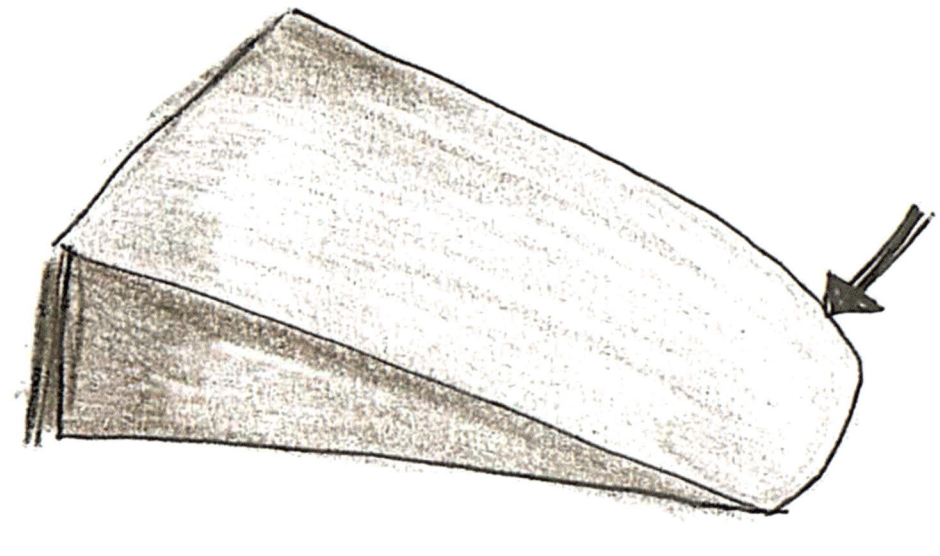

– Guess the meaning of the idiom in the dialogue below.

Suzie: Did you hear that Tim earned a lot of money from his Coin A investment?

Ben: I heard that. Whenever I hear that kind of news, I come to start doubting if it is worth it to work at a company. Should I invest my money to make more money like other people?

Suzie: Don't forget that people who make a fortune from Coin A investments are only a few. Most of them are losing their money. Some people must even be broke. Investments might make you richer, but it could be <u>the thin</u> end of the wedge, too.

L.M(표면적 의미)	F.M(비유적 의미)
wedge의 가는 끝부분	a first step along a path of increasingly damaging consequences; 심각한 일의 시작이 되는 일(행동)

– History: wedge는 돌이나 목재를 비틀어 떼어 내기 위해서 사용하는 V자 모양의 금속이나 목재 덩어리를 말하는데, 쐐기를 박으면 돌이나 목재가 깨지는 결과를 초래할 수 있다는 데에서 유래함.

♣ Make your own dialogue.

⊙ a **thorn** in the flesh/side

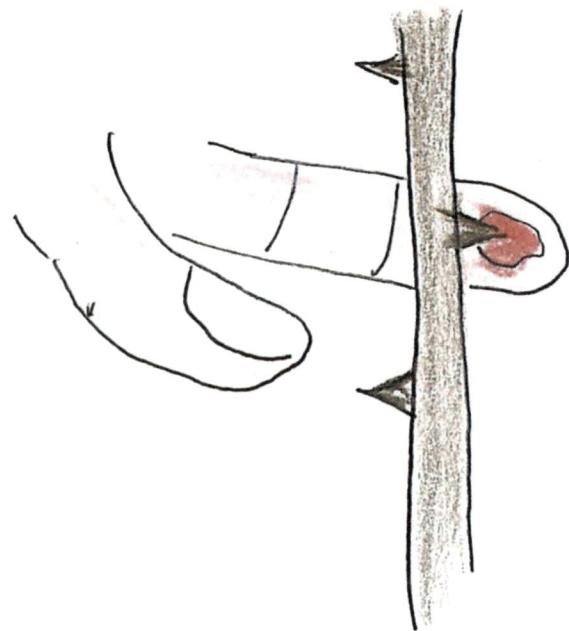

− Guess the meaning of the idiom in the dialogue below.

Suzie: How is Eddie doing nowadays?

Sunny: He seems to be going through puberty. He doesn't want to talk with me at all.

Suzie: A teenaged boy is a *thorn* in the flesh to their parents.

L.M(표면적 의미)	F.M(비유적 의미)
살 속에 박힌 가시	a person or thing which causes persistent pain or annoyance; 골칫거리, 고민거리

− History: 구약성서에서는 이스라엘이 가나안을 침략하려고 준비했을 때, 신이 모세를 통해서 그들이 모든 거주자를 내보내야 한다고 명령하셨는데, 따르지 않고 남는 자는 고통을 겪게 될 것이라고 말하였음. 신약성서에서는 사도 바울이 예수에 의지하고 겸손을 유지하기 위해서 가시가 박힌 고통(고질병에 걸렸음)을 이야기한 데에서 유래함.

♣ Make your own dialogue.

⊙ to hang by a **thread**

– Guess the meaning of the idiom in the dialogue below.

Suzie: Don't doze off at the wheel. Just pull over your car. I will drive the car instead of you.

Ben: Sorry. I feel drowsy after eating too much.

Suzie: I don't want us to hang by a *thread*.

L.M(표면적 의미)	F.M(비유적 의미)
실오라기 하나로 매달리다	to be in a perilous state; 위험한 상황에 있는

– History: 디오니시오스 왕에게 아첨했던 다모클레스의 머리 위에 머리카락 한 올로 칼을 매달아 둠으로써 칼이 떨어져 그에게 언제라도 위험이 닥칠 수 있게 되었다는 데에서 유래함.

♣ Make your own dialogue.

⊙ to give someone the thumbs up/down

to give someone the thumbs up/down

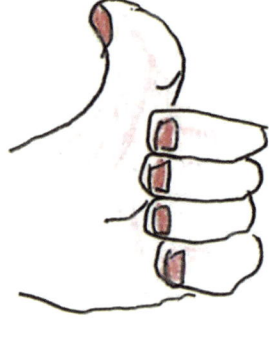
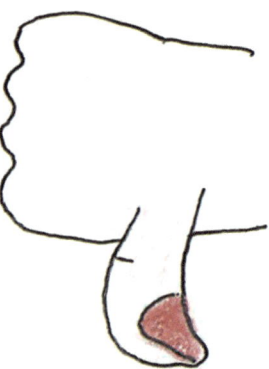

- Guess the meaning of the idiom in the dialogue below.

Suzie: My mom finally <u>gave me the **thumbs** up</u> about sleeping over at Sunny's house.

Ben: Does she know that boys were also invited to that party?

Suzie: No! She knows that it's a girls-only party. Never spill the beans to my mom.

L.M(표면적 의미)	F.M(비유적 의미)
누군가에게 엄지를 들어 올리다/내리다	to show approval/disapproval of something; 어떤 사안에 대한 승인/거부를 보여 주다

- History: 로마 시대에 검투사(gladiators) 결투를 보고 왕이 엄지를 올리고 내림으로써 그들의 생존과 죽음의 운명을 결정하였다는 데에서 유래함.

♣ Make your own dialogue.

◉ to steal someone's thunder

– Guess the meaning of the idiom in the dialogue below.

Ben: Did you decide what to write about on your final project for the vocabulary class?

Suzie: I'm thinking about writing about idioms.

Ben: Really? As far as I heard, Tim will also write about that, too.

Suzie: What? When I asked him about the topic for the project, he told me that he hadn't decided it yet.

Ben: Did you tell him about your topic, then? It seems like he <u>stole your thunder.</u>

L.M(표면적 의미)	F.M(비유적 의미)
누군가의 천둥을 훔치다	to upstage someone, to take the credit properly belonging to someone else; 누군가가 받아야 할 관심/인기/인정을 가로채다/선수 치다

– History: 극작가였던 John Dennis가 자신의 연극에서 드라마틱한 천둥소리의 음향 효과를 내기 위해서 깡통 소리를 이용하였는데, 연극 자체는 혹평으로 일찍 막을 내림. 얼마 되지 않아 Macbeth라는 연극에서 Dennis가 발명한 천둥소리를 사용했다는 것을 알고 불같이 화를 내며 "내 연극은 일찍 막을 내리게 하고, 감히 허락도 없이 내가 발명한 음향 효과를 사용하다니…."라고 말한 데에서 유래함.

♣ Make your own dialogue.

⊙ to tie the knot

- Guess the meaning of the idiom in the dialogue below.

Suzie: Finally Sam and Yumi *tied* the knot.

Ben: Wish them a happy marriage life!

L.M(표면적 의미)	F.M(비유적 의미)
매듭을 묶다	to get married; 결혼하다

- History: 1. "혀로 만든 매듭은 치아로 끊을 수 없다"라는 16세기의 옛 격언에서 유래한 말로, 결혼 이라는 쉽게 맺어진 유대 관계는 쉽게 풀어질 수 없다는 경고를 뜻한다고 함.
  2. 과거의 몇몇 부족들이 결혼할 때 신랑과 신부의 옷을 당겨서 매듭을 짓던 풍습에서 유래함.
  3. 옛날 가난했던 반지살 돈이 없었던 가난한 농부가 반지 대신 가느다란 실을 손가락 에 묶어준 데서 유래함.

♣ **Make your own dialogue.**

⊙ to tilt at windmills

- Guess the meaning of the idiom in the dialogue below.

Suzie: What do think about Tom's future plan?

Ben: Too promising to accomplish. He is a person who *tilts* at windmills.

L.M(표면적 의미)	F.M(비유적 의미)
풍차를 기울어지게 하다	to face an imagined evil, to pursue an ideal with little hope of its realisation; 상상의 악마/괴물에 맞서다, 현실의 희망이 거의 없는 상태에서 이상을 추구하다

- History: 세르반테스의 돈키호테의 장면으로, 풍차가 거대한 괴물이라며 공격하다가 풍차의 날개에 창이 걸려 땅바닥으로 굴러떨어졌다는 데에서 유래함.

♣ Make your own dialogue.

Idioms from A to Z: T

⊙ in the nick of **time**

– Guess the meaning of the idiom in the dialogue below.

Suzie: The traffic jam was too terrible.
Ben: Were you late for work?
Suzie: No. I just got there <u>in the nick of *time*.</u>

L.M(표면적 의미)	F.M(비유적 의미)
정확한 그 시간(자리)에	at exactly the right moment; at the very last minute, only just in time; 아슬아슬하게 때를 맞추어, 바로 그 순간

– History: 지금은 사장된 단어인 '목표로 하는 정확한 자리(자국)'를 뜻하는 nick에서 유래한 말로, 어떤 일이 일어나거나 됐어야 하는 정확한 그 시간(자리)을 뜻하는 데에서 유래함.

♣ Make your own dialogue.

⊙ to toe the line

- Guess the meaning of the idiom in the dialogue below.

Suzie: I don't like the new school rules.

Ben: Me neither, but we have to *toe* the line. Rules are rules….

L.M(표면적 의미)	F.M(비유적 의미)
라인에 발가락을 딛고 서다	to submit to authority, regulations; 규칙에 따르다, 위에서 시키는 대로 하다

- History: 달리기 경주에서 모든 참가자들은 출발선에 발가락을 두는 규칙에 따라야 했다는 데에서 유래함.

♣ Make your own dialogue.

⊙ tit for tat

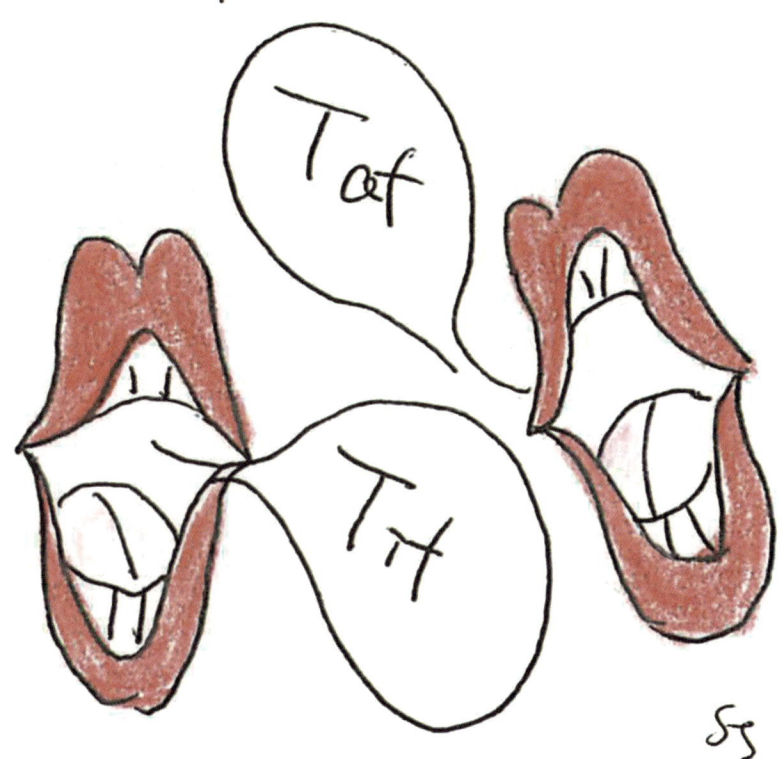

— Guess the meaning of the idiom in the dialogue below.

Suzie: I am upset about William.

Ben: What for?

Suzie: I asked him for help with a party preparation, but he just denied my request.

Ben: He must be busy.

Suzie: Not that I know of. I won't help him even if he asks me for help later. It's <u>tit</u> for <u>tat</u>.

L.M(표면적 의미)	F.M(비유적 의미)
수도꼭지에 대한 팁	retaliation, the exchange of blow for blow, insult for insult, etc; 복수, 타격에는 타격으로 응수하다

— History: 15세기에 쓰였던 두음법칙의 표현이던 'tip for tap'이 변형되어 16세기부터 사용되었다고 함.

♣ **Make your own dialogue.**

⊙ to grow like Topsy

- Guess the meaning of the idiom in the dialogue below.

Suzie: James is sometimes out of control.

Ben: He grew like Topsy, I guess.

L.M(표면적 의미)	F.M(비유적 의미)
Topsy처럼 자라다(성장하다)	to grow without attention, or help; 주의나 보살핌 없이 자라나다, 계획하지 않은 대로 빨리 자라다

- History: 유대 제도를 반대하는 소설인 *Uncle Tom's Cabin*(톰 삼촌의 오두막)에 나오는 작고 생기발랄한 노예 소녀인 Topsy가 어디서 태어났고 부모가 누구인지에 관한 질문에 답하기를 거부하는 대화에서 유래함.

♣ Make your own dialogue.

⊙ **touch** wood

- Guess the meaning of the idiom in the dialogue below.

Suzie: I feel like I won't pass the interview.
Ben: Just *touch* wood. Think positively until you hear the result.

L.M(표면적 의미)	F.M(비유적 의미)
나무를 만지다	words spoken to avoid bad luck and be blessed with good luck; 부정을 피하고 행운을 빌기 위해서 말하여진 표현.

- History: 영국에서는 나무를 'touch' 하거나, 미국에서는 나무를 'knock' 하는 행위가 부정 타는 것을 물리친다는 데에서 유래했다고 함.

♣ Make your own dialogue.

⊙ to come up/ turn up trumps

- Guess the meaning of the idiom in the dialogue below.

Suzie: How did the negotiation go with your boss?
Ben: I guess I <u>came up *trumps*</u> on that. I'm looking forward to a wage increase.

L.M(표면적 의미)	F.M(비유적 의미)
트럼프 카드를 보여 주다	unexpectedly to produce just what is needed at the last moment, to turn out well after all; 기대 이상의 효과를 거두다, 예상외로 잘하다

- History: Trump는 triumph(승리)에서 변형되어 사용된 말로, 카드 게임에서 다른 카드 패보다 점수가 높아서 가지고 있으면 좋은 우승패임. 따라서 'trump 카드'를 가지고 있다가 제시하면 게임의 판세가 유리하게 돌아가는 데에서 유래함.

♣ Make your own dialogue.

◉ to talk turkey

- Guess the meaning of the idiom in the dialogue below.

Suzie: Everyone is here, so let's _talk turkey_ from now.
Ben: Okay. What issue should we start talking first?

L.M(표면적 의미)	F.M(비유적 의미)
칠면조 얘기를 하다	to get down to business, to discuss frankly; 솔직히 얘기하다, 본격적으로 착수하다

- History: 미국의 백인과 원주민들이 함께 사냥을 한 뒤에 사냥감을 나누는 과정에서, 백인이 원주민들에게 "내가 칠면조를 가지면, 네가 독수리를 가져가고, 아니면 내가 독수리를 가지면, 네가 칠면조를 가져가라."라고 말하자, 위트 넘치던 원주민이 "(독수리 얘기 말고) 칠면조 얘기나 합시다."라고 말한 데에서 유래함.

♣ Make your own dialogue.

Idioms from A to Z: U, V

-U, V-

♣ These are the List of Idioms U and V. Are there any idioms you already know? If not, try to guess the meaning of the idioms below.

- **up** and running ⸺⸺⸺⸺⸺⸺⸺⸺⸺⸺⸺⸺ ☐
- an **ugly** duckling ⸺⸺⸺⸺⸺⸺⸺⸺⸺⸺⸺ ☐
- the **upper** crust ⸺⸺⸺⸺⸺⸺⸺⸺⸺⸺⸺ ☐
- to have/get/gain the **upper** hand ⸺⸺⸺⸺⸺⸺ ☐

- **vale** of tears ⸺⸺⸺⸺⸺⸺⸺⸺⸺⸺⸺⸺ ☐
- to draw a **veil** over ⸺⸺⸺⸺⸺⸺⸺⸺⸺⸺ ☐
- a **vicious** circle ⸺⸺⸺⸺⸺⸺⸺⸺⸺⸺⸺ ☐

◉ up and running

- Guess the meaning of the idiom in the dialogue below.

Suzie: Thank you for getting my computer fixed.
Ben: Don't mention it. How is it working?
Suzie: *Up and running.*
Ben: Good to hear that!

L.M(표면적 의미)	F.M(비유적 의미)
정상적으로 작동하는	functioning as it ought, operating without defect; 결함 없이 잘 작동하는

- History: 컴퓨터를 사용했던 초기 시절에는 자주 다운되고 작동을 멈추는 것으로 악명이 높았기 때문에 컴퓨터 기술자들이 고치면 고치자마자 다시 작동을 시작했다는 데에서 유래함.

♣ Make your own dialogue.

◉ an ugly duckling

- Guess the meaning of the idiom in the dialogue below.

Suzie: Don't you think the main actor in this movie is such a beauty?

Ben: I think so, too. She is not only pretty but also smart.

Suzie: What is interesting is she used to be an ugly duckling when she was a little child.

Ben: Unbelievable!

L.M(표면적 의미)	F.M(비유적 의미)
미운 오리 새끼	a gauche, awkward child who blossoms into a beauty; 부자연스럽고 어색하였으나 나중에 아름다움을 꽃 피우는 아이

- History: 안데르센 동화 *The Ugly Duckling*(미운 오리 새끼)에서 나온 사고로 오리알에 섞여 들어간 백조의 새끼가 다른 생김으로 놀림을 받다가 겨울을 지나고 멋진 백조로 거듭났다는 이야기에서 유래함.

♣ Make your own dialogue.

⊙ the upper crust

- Guess the meaning of the idiom in the dialogue below.

Suzie: James is from **the upper crust**, but he is penniless.
Ben: What happened to him?
Suzie: He failed in investing in stocks.

L.M(표면적 의미)	F.M(비유적 의미)
위쪽의 딱딱한 부분	the aristocracy, higher social circles; 귀족인, 높은 사회 계층

- History: 빵의 윗부분은 오븐 바닥에 닿지 않았는데 이 부분은 빵의 가장 좋은 부분으로 비유적으로 표현된 데에서 유래함.

♣ Make your own dialogue.

◉ to have/get/gain the upper hand

– Guess the meaning of the idiom in the dialogue below.

Suzie: What does the "bandwagon effect" mean?

Ben: That means a phenomenon in which votes are drawn to candidates who have the *upper* hand in election campaigns.

Suzie: I see.

L.M(표면적 의미)	F.M(비유적 의미)
손의 위쪽 부위를 잡다	to gain the advantage, to win control; 우위를 차지하다

– History: 술 마시기 또는 도박 게임에서 유래한 것으로, 게임의 참가자는 막대기의 가장 아래 부분을 잡으면 그 사람 다음 참가자는 바로 윗부분을 잡는 방식으로 진행이 되고, 가장 높은 (top) 부분을 잡는 사람이 승자가 된다는 데에서 유래함.

♣ Make your own dialogue.

⊙ vale of tears

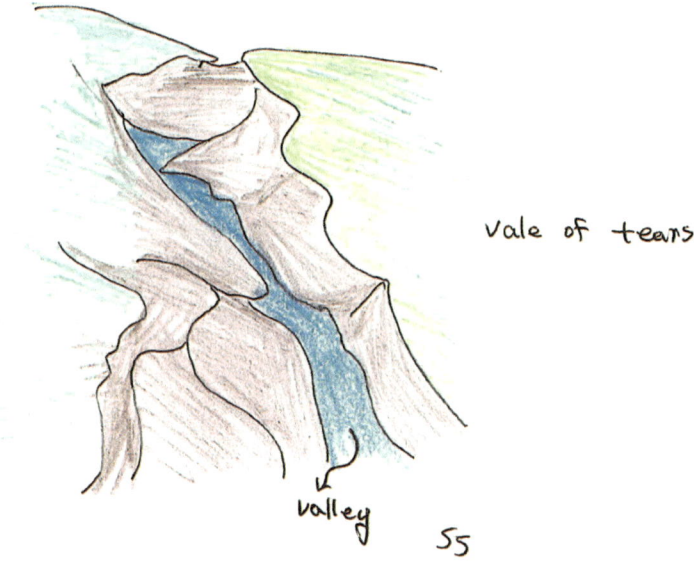

– Guess the meaning of the idiom in the dialogue below.

Ben: Deepest condolences for your loss.

Suzie: Thank you. Life is indeed a *vale of tears*.

L.M(표면적 의미)	F.M(비유적 의미)
눈물의 계곡	life with all its troubles and sorrows; 모든 고민거리와 슬픔이 가득한 삶(인생)

– History: 산꼭대기와 계곡은 감정의 기복을 묘사하는 데 오랜 시간 동안 사용됐음. Valley of tears는 Valley of Baca(Weeping)으로, 성경의 시편에 언급되었는데, 예루살렘으로 이동하던 중 건넜던 매우 건조한 지역(땅)을 가리킴.

♣ **Make your own dialogue.**

◉ to draw a veil over

to draw a veil over

- Guess the meaning of the idiom in the dialogue below.

Ben: Tim got caught cheating during the final exam.
Suzie: The worse thing is he tried to draw a veil over it when he was caught.
Ben: He should have realized that honesty is the best policy.

L.M(표면적 의미)	F.M(비유적 의미)
베일(면사포)로 내려서 가리다	to avoid discussing, to hush up; 유야무야로 덮다/숨기다

- History: 수치스러운 물건이나 장면을 베일(면사포) 뒤에 신중하게 가리는 데에서 유래함.

♣ Make your own dialogue.

⊙ a **vicious** **circle**

- Guess the meaning of the idiom in the dialogue below.

Ben: It's tiring to pay back interests on the bank.

Suzie: It's like a <u>vicious circle.</u> To pay back interests, you borrow money, and it becomes another debt. I hope you will break out of the vicious circle sooner or later.

L.M(표면적 의미)	F.M(비유적 의미)
악의적인 순환	one difficulty leading to another, which aggravates the first; a downward spiral of negative reactions; 어떤 한 어려움이 또 다른 어려움으로 이끌다

- History: 로직(논리)은 악순환의 개념을 갖고 있는데, A가 B에 영향을 주면 B는 C에 영향을 주고 다시 이는 A에 영향을 준다. 따라서 A라는 행위나 사건이 B의 반응을 일으키고, B는 A를 더 나쁘게 만든다.

♣ Make your own dialogue.

Idioms from A to Z: W

- W -

♣ These are the List of Idioms W. Are there any idioms you already know? If not, try to guess the meaning of the idioms below.

- on the **wagon** -- ☐
- to go to the **wall** (= to have one's back to the **wall**) -------- ☐
- on the **warpath** -- ☐
- to meet one's **Waterloo** ------------------------------ ☐
- **warts** and all -- ☐
- to fall by the **wayside** ------------------------------- ☐
- to pull one's **weight** --------------------------------- ☐
- to separate the **wheat** from the chaff ------------------ ☐
- a **whipping** boy -------------------------------------- ☐
- a **white** elephant ------------------------------------- ☐

- to do something **willy-nilly** ---------------------------- ☐
- a **wild** goose chase ---------------------------------- ☐
- to take someone under one's **wing** --------------------- ☐
- a **wet** blanket --- ☐
- a **wolf** in sheep's clothing ---------------------------- ☐
- to cry **wolf** --- ☐
- to have got out of the **wrong** side of the bed ------------- ☐
- to pull the **wool** over someone's eyes ------------------- ☐

⊙ on the wagon

- Guess the meaning of the idiom in the dialogue below.

Ben: I saw Tom drinking alcohol at the bar last night.
Suzie: What? I remember his new year's resolution was <u>on the *wagon*</u>. Too bad!

L.M(표면적 의미)	F.M(비유적 의미)
마차 위에(서)	teetotal, abstaining from drinking alcohol; 금주의

- History: 원래 'on the water wagon'에서 유래된 말로, 당시에 거리의 마른 먼지를 적시기 위해서 마차에 물통을 싣고 뿌리곤 했는데, 마차에 금주에 대해서 같이 홍보하기도 했다고 함. 스스로 금주하겠다고 선언/약속한 사람들이 마차에 올라타서 금주 홍보를 했다는 데에서 마차 위에 올라타면 금주를, 다시 내리면 다시 술을 마신다는 것을 의미하게 됨. 유명한 미국의 시트콤인 *Seinfield* 시리즈 중 Season 3 Episode 29에서는 "On the Wagon, Off the Wagon"이란 주제로 이 이디엄이 사용됨.

♣ **Make your own dialogue.**

⊙ to go to the wall (= to have one's back to the wall)

- Guess the meaning of the idiom in the dialogue below.

Ben: How is your school project going?
Suzie: I'm trying to doing my best, but I feel like I will go to the wall in the end.
Ben: Don't say that! You can do it. If you need any help, just feel free to ask me.
Suzie: Thanks.

L.M(표면적 의미)	F.M(비유적 의미)
벽 쪽으로 가다	to give way under pressure, to suffer failure, ruin; 실패하다

- History: 막다른 골목으로 향해 가는 사람은 종국에 가서는 벽에 부딪히게 된다는 데에서 유래함.

♣ Make your own dialogue.

⦿ on the warpath

- Guess the meaning of the idiom in the dialogue below.

Ben: Tom hasn't returned my book yet since he borrowed it last month.
Suzie: Oh my gosh! Again?
Ben: I am on the warpath now.
Suzie: Anyway, you need to have a serious talk about that issue with him.

L.M(표면적 의미)	F.M(비유적 의미)
출정의 길 위에(서)	spoiling for a fight, in an aggressive or vengeful mood; 화가 나서 싸우려 하는, 전쟁에 임박하다

- History: 북미 원주민(인디언)들 사이에서 유래한 말로, 호전적인 부족이 적과 맞서러 가는 도중에 택하는 길을 가리킴

♣ Make your own dialogue.

⊙ to meet one's Waterloo

− Guess the meaning of the idiom in the dialogue below.

Ben: Did you watch the baseball game between LG and OB?

Suzie: It turned out totally the opposite result of what I thought. I thought OB would win by a mile.

Ben: Yeah, that's what I expected, too. I think OB met its *Waterloo* in the last game.

L.M(표면적 의미)	F.M(비유적 의미)
누군가의 워털루를 맞닥뜨리다	to suffer defeat after initial success; 초기의 성공 이후로 대패하다(큰 패배를 맛보다)

− History: 워털루에서 연합군에 의해서 크게 대패한 나폴레옹의 일화에서 유래함.

♣ Make your own dialogue.

⊙ warts and all

- Guess the meaning of the idiom in the dialogue below.

Ben: How was your vacation in Cancun?

Suzie: Well, actually the hotel I stayed in had some run-down parts, but I liked it _warts_ and all.

Ben: I see. Since Covid is lasting longer than we expected, I would feel the same as you where ever I went as long as I could go abroad.

L.M(표면적 의미)	F.M(비유적 의미)
결점(혹)과 모든 것	no attempt to hide defects; 흠/결함을 숨기려는 노력/시도 하지 않는/있는 그대로

- History: 옛날에는 권력자의 초상화를 그릴 때 흠을 가리고 좀 더 멋지게 그리는 관습이 있었는데, Oliver Cromwell은 화가에게 자신과 얼굴의 점, 주름, 사마귀 등 있는 그대로 똑같이 그리지 않으면 그림에 대한 대가를 지급하지 않겠다고 말한 데에서 유래함.

♣ **Make your own dialogue.**

⦿ to fall by the **wayside**

- Guess the meaning of the idiom in the dialogue below.

Ben: How did the audition go?

Suzie: I think it fell by the *wayside.*

Ben: Sorry to hear that.

L.M(표면적 의미)	F.M(비유적 의미)
길가에 떨어지다	to drop out; to fail; 실패하다

- History: 예수께서 씨 뿌리는 사람을 언급한 우화에서 유래함. 일부 씨앗은 좋은 토양에 떨어지지만, 일부는 가시나 돌밭 또는 길가에 떨어진다고 말하였음. 씨앗은 하나님의 말씀을 의미하는데, 토양의 다른 종류는 그 말씀을 듣는 사람들의 태도를 의미함.

♣ Make your own dialogue.

⊙ to pull one's **weight**

- Guess the meaning of the idiom in the dialogue below.

Ben: A surprise party for Sam's birthday is coming up. We need to prepare for it.

Suzie: Let's make up a to-do-list and then pull our *weight* for it.

L.M(표면적 의미)	F.M(비유적 의미)
무게를 실어 당기다	to do one's fair share; 본분을 다하다/ 공평하게 분담하다

- History: 노 젓기에서 유래한 것으로, 모든 선원은 자신의 몸무게에 맞춰 효과적으로 노를 저어야 한다고 함.

♣ Make your own dialogue.

⊙ to separate the wheat from the chaff

to separate the wheat from the chaff

SJ

— Guess the meaning of the idiom in the dialogue below.

Ben: We are living in a flood of information. The problem is that there is too much fake news around us.

Suzie: I think students should get media literacy education to <u>separate the wheat from the chaff</u>.

L.M(표면적 의미)	F.M(비유적 의미)
곡물과 겉껍질을 구분하다	to separate the good from the bad, the valuable from the worthless; 좋은 것과 나쁜 것, 가치 있는 것과 가치 없는 것을 구분하다

— History: 좋은 곡물과 쓸데없는 겉껍질을 구분해 내기 위해서 옥수수 등을 탈곡하는 과정에서 유래함.

♣ Make your own dialogue.

⊙ a **whipping boy**

a whipping boy

- Guess the meaning of the idiom in the dialogue below.

Ben: The rumor says that Tom's company will carry out a large-scale restructuring.

Suzie: Every employee hopes not to be a *whipping* boy this time.

L.M(표면적 의미)	F.M(비유적 의미)
채찍질 맞는 소년	one who suffers the punishment for the wrongdoing of another, a scapegoat; 희생양

- History: 17세기 중반부터 사용된 표현으로, 잘못된 행동에 대해서 책망을 듣는 사람을 비유할 때 쓰임. 'a whipping boy'는 당시 궁에서 왕자와 함께 탁아 시설과 교실(공부방)을 사용하 였는데, 왕자가 잘못된 행동을 할 때마다 왕자 대신에 매를 맞는 역할을 하였다고 함.

♣ Make your own dialogue.

♣ a white elephant

- Guess the meaning of the idiom in the dialogue below.

Ben: I don't ride this electric bike anymore. It's like a **white** elephant to me now.

Suzie: Why don't you sell it at the used market?

Ben: What a great idea!

L.M(표면적 의미)	F.M(비유적 의미)
흰 코끼리	an unwanted object of no great use or value; 별 쓸모나 가치가 없는 원치 않는 물건

- History: 동남아시아에서 하얀 코끼리는 권력을 뜻하는 신성한 동물로 여겨졌는데, 그 코끼리의 죽음은 재난을 예고하였음. 이 코끼리를 관리하는 데에는 많은 돈이 쓰였으며, 노동으로 사용할 수도 없었기 때문에 결국엔 점차 주인을 망하게 만들었다는 부정적 의미가 생김.

♣ Make your own dialogue.

⊙ to do something **willy-nilly**

— Guess the meaning of the idiom in the dialogue below.

Suzie: Would you like to do part-time work as a teaching assistant?
Ben: Yes!
Suzie: Keep in mind that this shouldn't be done willy-nilly.
Ben: Okay. Thanks.

L.M(표면적 의미)	F.M(비유적 의미)
원하건 원하지 않건 무언가를 하다	to do something whether one likes it or not; 원하건 원치 않건 하는/싫건 좋건

— History: 17세기 초에 생긴 말로, will은 뭔가를 하려는 의지를 나타내는 동사이고 'nill'은 지금은 사라진 말이지만, 'will'과 반대되는 의미를 지녔다고 함. 원하건 원하지 않건 어떤 일이 필연적으로 일어날 것이라는 의미로 이어짐.

♣ Make your own dialogue.

Idioms from A to Z: W

⊙ a wild goose chase

– Guess the meaning of the idiom in the dialogue below.

Suzie: I need to go on a diet before my summer vacation begins.

Ben: Again? You seemed to keep failing at it.

Suzie: Don't discourage me!

Ben: I mean you need to make a plan first to succeed it this time. It will be <u>a wild goose chase</u> without it.

L.M(표면적 의미)	F.M(비유적 의미)
야생 기러기 뒤쫓기	a purposeless errand, a pointless exercise, a waste of time: 목적 없는 일(심부름), 의미 없는 운동, 시간 낭비 등

– History: 16세기 후반에 말을 타고 하는 경기 중, 기수가 그의 뜻대로 방향을 바꾸며 무작위로 코스를 만들면 다른 참가자들이 똑같이 따라가려고 했었는데, 이는 마치 야생 기러기들이 앞에서 이끄는 기러기 뒤를 뒤따라가는 것을 연상시켰다고 함. 셰익스피어는 이 문구를 로미오와 줄리엣에서 인용하였음.

♣ **Make your own dialogue.**

⊙ to take someone under one's wing

- Guess the meaning of the idiom in the dialogue below.

Ben: How is the preparation for studying abroad going?
Suzie: Pretty good!
Ben: Is there anyone who <u>takes you under his/her **wing**</u> there?
Suzie: Fortunately, my aunt on my mother's side lives near my school.
Ben: Good for you.

L.M(표면적 의미)	F.M(비유적 의미)
누군가를 자신의 날개 아래에 두다	돌보다(보살피다); 감싸서 보호하다

- History: 암탉이 자신의 어린 병아리들을 자신의 날개 아래에 감싸 보호하는 것으로 13세기 이래로 많은 영문학에서 인용되었음. 하지만 훨씬 오래전으로 거슬러 올라가면 이 비유의 역사는 신약성서의 Matthew 23:37에서 예수님께서 한탄하시며 말씀하신 구절에 사용되기 시작하여 성경의 권위 덕분으로 수 세기를 지나 오늘날까지도 많이 사용되고 있음.
"너희는 예언자들을 죽인다! 너희는 너희에게 보내진 사람들에게 돌을 던진다! 암탉이 자신의 새끼를 날개 아래 감싸 보호하듯이 내가 얼마나 자주 너희들을 불러 모았던가!"

♣ **Make your own dialogue.**

⊙ a wet blanket

- Guess the meaning of the idiom in the dialogue below.

Suzie: What do you think of Sam's joke?

Ben: I think his joke are too terrible. They are usually out of date.

Suzie: I hate to say it…, but he is such a *wet* blanket.

L.M(표면적 의미)	F.M(비유적 의미)
젖은 담요	흥을 깨는 (분위기를 망치는) 사람

- History: 야외에 캠핑을 할 때 밤이 되면 불을 피워 캠핑의 즐거움의 절정을 맞이하는데, 캠프파이어를 끝내기 위해 불을 끌 때 보통 담요나 이불에 물을 적셔서 불 위에 던졌다는 데에서 유래함. 젖은 담요나 이불을 던지는 행위는 즐거운 캠프파이어의 시간이 끝나간다는 것을 암시하기 때문에 젖은 담요가 즐거운 분위기나 흥을 깨는 사람으로 의미하게 되었음.

♣ Make your own dialogue.

⊙ a wolf in sheep's clothing

a wolf in sheep's clothing

- Guess the meaning of the idiom in the dialogue below.

Suzie: I think the new boss is kind and gentle.

Ben: Beware of him. He seems generous, but the rumor is that he's <u>a wolf in sheep's clothing.</u>

L.M(표면적 의미)	F.M(비유적 의미)
양의 탈(옷)을 쓴 늑대	양가죽을 쓴 늑대; (온화함을 가장한) 위선자

- History: 이솝 우화에 나오는 양털을 뒤집어쓰고 양인 척하는 탐욕스러운 늑대를 가리킴. 이 이야기는 고대 지중해 쪽 문명에서 아주 유명했다고 함. 예수님도 Matthew 7:15에서 비유적인 이야기로 인용하였음.
"양의 옷을 입었지만, 실상은 굶주린 늑대와 같은, 네게 접근하는 거짓된 예언자를 경계하여라!"

♣ Make your own dialogue.

⊙ to cry wolf

- Guess the meaning of the idiom in the dialogue below.

Suzie: If you did something wrong, just tell me honestly. Honesty is the best policy. If you cry wolf again, no one will come to help you.

Ben: I will promise not to lie to you again!

L.M(표면적 의미)	F.M(비유적 의미)
늑대라고 소리치다	도와달라고 소란을 피우다(도움이 꼭 필요하지 않으면서 소란을 피워 정작 도움이 필요할 때는 사람들이 믿지 않게 됨); 거짓 경보

- History: 평소 마을 사람들에게 "늑대가 나타났어요!"라고 소리치면 마을 주민들이 달려와 도와주려고 했던 것을 즐겼던 한 양치기 소년의 이야기를 다룬 이솝 우화 중 하나임. 어느 날, 막상 실제로 늑대가 나타나서 소년이 도움을 요청했음에도 사람들은 이번에도 거짓인 것으로 알고 아무도 도와주러 오지 않았음. 이 이야기는 19세기 중반부터 사용되기 시작하였으나, 인기 있는 책의 제목과 팝송의 제목으로도 사용될 만큼 많이 사용되고 있는 표현임.

♣ Make your own dialogue.

⊙ to have got out of the wrong side of the bed

- Guess the meaning of the idiom in the dialogue below.

Suzie: What's wrong with you? Did you get out of the *wrong* side of the bed today?

Ben: Yes, so be careful when you talk to me. I'm very emotionally sensitive today.

L.M(표면적 의미)	F.M(비유적 의미)
잘못된 방향으로 침대에서 일어나다	꿈자리가 나쁘다; 기분이 언짢다

- History: 침대의 잘못된 방향(쪽)은 왼쪽을 의미하는데, 로마인들의 믿음에 따르면, 왼쪽에 보이는 징조로써 불운이 나타나고 왼쪽과 관련된 것들은 악을 불러온다고 함. 비슷한 미신은 16세기와 17세기에 영국에도 있었는데 오른쪽으로 일어날 때 모든 일이 잘 풀린다고 함.

♣ Make your own dialogue.

◉ to pull the wool over someone's eyes

– Guess the meaning of the idiom in the dialogue below.

Suzie: Did you hear that Sam and Yumi broke up?

Ben: Really? What happened to them?

Suzie: Sam played games too much and lied to Yumi about it.

Ben: He keeps pulling the *wool* over her eyes, but this time it didn't work.

L.M(표면적 의미)	F.M(비유적 의미)
누군가의 눈 위를 양털로 씌우다(가리다)	남의 눈을 속이다

– History: 이 표현은 신사들이 가발을 착용했던 시대로 거슬러 올라감. 당시 머리를 우스꽝스럽게 '양털'이라고 불렀음. 소매치기 현장처럼 누군가가 봐서는 안 되는 무언가를 보지 못하게 하기 위해서 가발(양털)을 당겨 눈을 가리게 했다는 데에서 유래함. 19세기 초반부터 미국 언론과 미국 문학 작품에 많이 사용되었지만, 실제 더 많은 권위를 얻게 된 것은 영국의 판사들의 사례에서 기인함. 영국의 판사들은 재판에 참석할 때 가발(양털)을 착용하였는데, 변호사들이 확실한 증거(근거)가 없을 때, 자신의 솜씨 좋은 언변 기술로 판사를 속이려고 했다는 상황을 잘 나타냄.

♣ Make your own dialogue.

Idioms from A to Z: X, Y, Z

-X, Y, Z-

♣ These are the List of Idioms X, Y and Z. Are there any idioms you already know? If not, try to guess the meaning of the idioms below.

- ⊙ **X**-Factor -- ☐
- ⊙ **X** marks the spot ------------------------------------ ☐

- ⊙ **You** can't have **your** cake and topping, too. ------------ ☐
- ⊙ **yank** one's chain ------------------------------------ ☐

- ⊙ **zero** in on something / someone --------------------- ☐
- ⊙ **zip** one's lip -- ☐

⊙ X-Factor

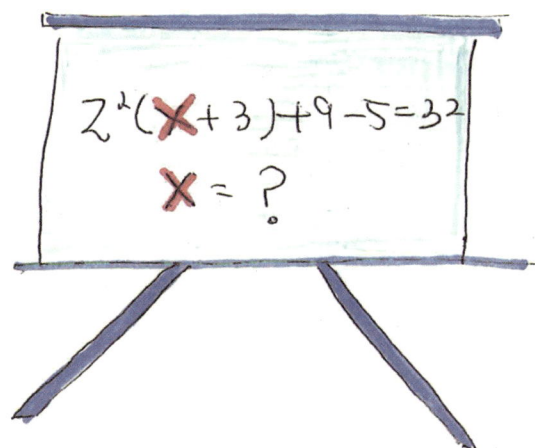

- Guess the meaning of the idiom in the dialogue below.

Suzie: Who won at the final stage?

Ben: Justin won. He is the X-Factor.

L.M(표면적 의미)	F.M(비유적 의미)
X인자(미지의 요인)	an outstanding extraordinary ability; 말로 표현이 안 되는 무언가가(특별함이) 있는,

- History: 대수학과 연관 있는 간단한 공식으로, 만약 하나의 미지수의 요인이 있으면 보통 그것은 X 인자로 정해짐. 즉, 'X 인자라는 것은 결론적으로 알 수 없는 것'으로 여겨졌으나, 최근에는 '형언할 수 없는 품질을 의미하는 것'으로 쓰이기 시작함. 이 이디엄을 타이틀로 영국에서는 유명한 프로듀서인 Simon Cowell이 TV 음악 경쟁 리얼리티 쇼를 제작하기도 하였음.

♣ Make your own dialogue.

◉ X marks the spot

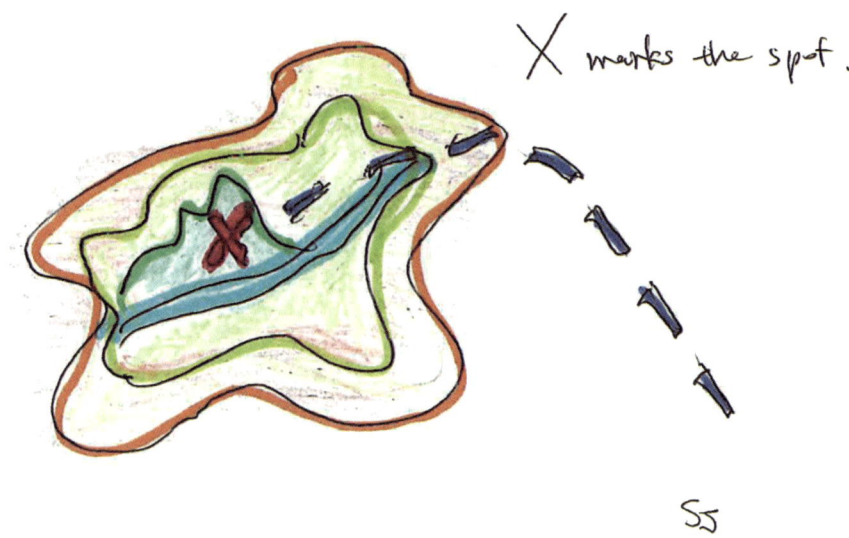

- Guess the meaning of the idiom in the dialogue below.

Suzie: Where is the restaurant we are looking for? We wandered around near here more than one hour.

Ben: It's strange. The map says X marks the spot.

L.M(표면적 의미)	F.M(비유적 의미)
그 자리에 X 표시를 하다	이곳이 바로 그곳이다; 정확한 장소

- History: 해적들의 지도에 보물의 위치에 X를 표시한 데에서 유래하였고, 영국 군대에서 사형을 시킬 사람의 심장에 검은 X가 쳐진 종이를 표시함으로써 처형했던 사례에서 일상적으로 많이 통용되었다고 함. 장교가 "X marks the spot"이라고 외치면, 군인들이 그 X를 향해 총을 쐈다고 함.

♣ Make your own dialogue.

◉ You can't have your cake and topping, too.

- Guess the meaning of the idiom in the dialogue below.

Ben: Did you decide where to go for your vacation?
Suzie: It's up in the air, still. I want to go to Hawaii and Barcelona.
Ben: <u>You can't have your cake and topping, too.</u> Choose one of two.

L.M(표면적 의미)	F.M(비유적 의미)
케이크와 토핑을 둘 다 가질 수는 없다	두 마리 토끼를 잡을 수 없다

- History: 원하는 것이 모순될 경우, 자신이 원하는 방식대로 모든 것을 가질 수는 없다는 이치에서 유래함. 같은 의미를 지닌 표현으로는 "You can't have your cake and eat it."이 있는데, 케이크를 일단 먹으면 먹은 부분은 사라져 버리기 때문에, 케이크를 보존하려면 케이크를 먹으면 안 된다는 이치에서 유래함.

♣ Make your own dialogue.

⊙ yank one's chain

- Guess the meaning of the idiom in the dialogue below.

Ben: Tom kept laughing at my photos from my old days.
Suzie: He likes **yanking** your chain.
Ben: He usually goes too far with the joke.

L.M(표면적 의미)	F.M(비유적 의미)
체인을 확 잡아당기다	누군가를 놀리다; 누군가에게 장난치다

- History: 금광에서 유래된 말로, 광부들은 화장실 변기로 레일이 달린 마차를 이용하였는데 마차가 움직이지 않도록 체인을 바퀴 앞에 두어 고정하였다고 함. 누군가 변기를 사용하는 동안 동료 광부들은 체인을 확 잡아당기는 장난을 치곤 했는데, 이때 변기를 사용하던 광부가 잡아당기지 말라고 경고하며 소리친 데에서 유래하였다고 함.

♣ Make your own dialogue.

⊙ zero in on something / someone

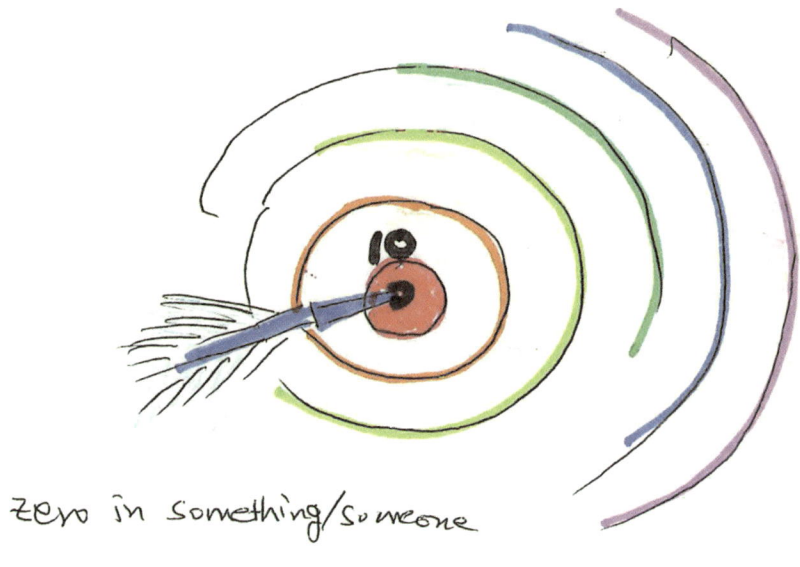

- Guess the meaning of the idiom in the dialogue below.

Ben: I need to raise my grade on the test for the vocabulary class.
Suzie: Try to **zero in on studying** for the test.

L.M(표면적 의미)	F.M(비유적 의미)
(계기 등을) 영(제로)에 맞추다	(총 따위의) 조준을 바로 잡다; …에 맞추다; 목표를 겨냥하다; 모든 관심(신경)을 집중시키다

- History: 서양의 오락 놀이 중 하나인 다트 게임이나 사격 또는 양궁을 할 때 가장 높은 점수인 10점 만점을 득하기 위해서는 정중앙의 빨간 원 안에 명중하여야 하는데, 그 빨강 원이 마치 숫자 0, 즉 zero와 비슷하게 생겼기 때문에 그 zero 안에 무언가를 꽂아 넣는다는 데에서 유래하였다는 것이 여러 가지 설 중의 하나임.

♣ Make your own dialogue.

⊙ zip one's lip

- Guess the meaning of the idiom in the dialogue below.

Ben: You never stop talking. _Zip your lip!_ I need a quiet time to focus on this.
Suzie: Sorry!

L.M(표면적 의미)	F.M(비유적 의미)
입술에 지퍼를 채우다	입 닫아! 쉿, 조용히 해!

- History: 1868년경에는 'Button your lips'이 사용되었는데, 이 시기에는 물건을 봉하기 위해서 단추가 사용되었기 때문이었음. 지퍼(zipper)가 발명되어 사용되기 시작하면서 단추(button)라는 단어 대신 지퍼(zipper)라는 단어가 관용구에 사용되었음.

♣ Make your own dialogue.